# Can't Wait for Sunday

# Can't Wait for Sunday

J. Michael Walters

wesleyan
publishing
house

Indianapolis, Indiana

Copyright © 2006 by Wesleyan Publishing House
Published by Wesleyan Publishing House
Indianapolis, Indiana 46250
Printed in the United States of America

ISBN 10: 0-89827-313-7
ISBN 13: 978-0-89827-313-7

All Scripture quotations, unless otherwise indicated, are taken from the *Holy Bible, New International Version*®. *NIV*®. Copyright 1973, 1978, 1984 by International Bible Society. Used by permission of Zondervan. All rights reserved.

The Scripture quotations herein marked RSV are from the *Revised Standard Version of the Bible*, copyright 1946, 1952, 1971 by the Division of Christian Education of the National Council of Churches of Christ in the USA. Used by permission.

Scripture quotations marked NASB are taken from the *New American Standard Bible*, © Copyright 1960, 1962, 1963, 1968, 1971, 1972, 1973, 1975, 1977, 1995 by The Lockman Foundation. Used by permission.

To the congregation of Houghton Church,
whose love of worship both inspired me and,
more importantly, transformed my life

# CONTENTS

—⁓—

# THE WEEKLY SPIN CYCLE

—ᘜᘴ—

*Worship is the center of the hourglass, the key to forming the inner-life of the church.*
—Robert Webber

## SILVER BULLET

By embracing the privilege of leading people in worship, pastors can thrive in a hectic and demanding vocation.

After twenty years in pastoral ministry, I've concluded that pastors inhabit a special dimension of time. Our week centers around Sunday, and every other day functions in relationship to the approaching Sabbath. Depending on how preparations for Sunday are progressing, our stress levels are either somewhat manageable or approaching that of an air traffic controller whose radar system has malfunctioned. Those outside ministry simply cannot know the anxiety that results from watching the calendar work its way inexorably through a week in which the sermon or order of service simply will not come into focus. When speaking to a group of pastors, I sometimes say, "On Thursday evening I went to sleep praying for a visit from the sermon fairies," then I watch as a look of instant understanding and empathy breaks over their faces. Pastors know exactly what I'm talking about.

Living in the weekly cycle of pastoral life—preparing sermons, ordering the service, composing bulletins, and generally pouring oneself into the primary public meeting of the church—takes its toll on pastors even under the best of circumstances. Yet living in this rhythmic cycle for more than two decades, I came to love it as much as anything I've ever done. That experience has made me a great advocate of both pastors and pastoral ministry. It is the best of all vocations. It is also an intensely difficult one. And the very thing that makes the pastorate exciting is also its greatest challenge—the worship of the church. Worship is never far from the center of the pastor's radar screen. It is the most public thing we do and one of the most important measures by which others evaluate our effectiveness. It is the rare pastor who can afford *not* to place great priority on preparing for Sunday worship.

Yet there are deeper concerns here than the pragmatic questions of church attendance and public approval. These are momentous days for the church. At no time in history have we experienced the kind of hostility from the popular culture that we now face. This makes the stakes for conducting public worship even higher than before. Our church members are immersed in a culture that devalues God, enthrones self, and is apathetic toward the things that we clergy contend are most important. Those cultural attitudes find their way into the church with frightening ease, where they leaven all aspects of ecclesial life, especially worship. The consumerist hunger for immediate payback, for example, has greatly complicated every conscientious pastor's task in leading worship. That makes it imperative that pastors both understand and commit themselves to implementing a biblically and theologically sound approach to worship, lest they be swept away by the powerful forces of an a-theistic culture.[1] And there is a great deal to be gained. In an age when religious faith is being questioned in almost every venue, it is through vital and culturally aware worship that congregations can thrive, finding their way amid hostile surroundings. Pastors who have the know-how, resources, and—most of all—the deep convictions to bring creative leadership to worship will have a significant advantage in ministering amid the culture of this age. That's why it is important for pastors to think biblically, theologically, and reflectively about the worship life of their churches.

As a pastoral theologian, I call pastors to engage this challenge, fully aware of the resources they have to marshal on behalf of the historic Christian faith. Liturgical scholar Don Saliers reminds us that "the continuing worship of God in the assembly is a form of theology. In fact, it is 'primary theology.' Worship in all of its social-cultural idioms is a theological act."[2] Saliers's words are a reminder that the purest theologians in our midst are those who give leadership to our churches—that is, pastors. There is much to lament about the divide that has sometimes existed between theology in the academy and theology in the parish, but at the very top of the list is the way such a divorce undermines the pastor's ability to lead congregational worship. The role of theology is to inform and assist the church in the fulfillment of her mission. This is no time for pastors and theologians to be at opposite ends of the room. What both groups have to say both to each another and to the world outside matters too much to allow intramural quarreling to suspend the conversation. French philosopher Simone Weil said, "To be always relevant, you have to say things which are eternal."[3] While both theologians and pastors can talk about the eternal, it is pastors who have the most important venue from which to speak on that invaluable theme.

This book is written primarily for pastors, although anyone involved in the worship life of the church may profit from it. Although my primary vocation in this stage of my life is that of college professor, I write as a pastor. As a pastoral theologian, I am most concerned with how theology affects the church and those who serve it. So in these pages, I dialogue with those who inhabit the weekly spin cycle of pastoral life. I have taught liturgical theology for ten years at both the undergraduate and graduate levels, and my students have been a continual source of inspiration and illumination to me. But more than anything else, my views on worship have been forged by decades-long experience at planning the Sunday service and by the many conversations, both formal and informal, I've had with ministerial peers.

This book will be helpful to pastors serving in nearly any setting, but it is written particularly with those from the revivalist tradition in mind. In this tradition worship is often employed as a tool for evangelism. The sermon and, more so in bygone days, the altar call dominate the order of service while the deeper dimensions of worship are often neglected. I observe that many pastors in this tradition—which happens to be my own—are now either trying to replicate an approach to worship what flourished in the 1950s and '60s or else have become wholly pragmatic, offering as worship whatever is most in sync with popular culture and, therefore, most likely to attract attention. Both of these approaches are misguided and unlikely to produce vital congregations that will be missional forces for the kingdom of God in the twenty-first century. This book points out a different course. I have distilled the principles set forth in this book into concise statements placed at the head of each chapter. Each concept is labeled a silver bullet, which may be an appropriate term given the language of hostility that has surrounded worship in the past couple of decades. While I hope these principles will be helpful to those in ministry, they are not presented as easy solutions to the complex problems facing the church.

My understanding of the theory and practice of worship has been profoundly shaped by the likes of Robert Webber, William Willimon, Eugene Peterson, and Marva Dawn. Beyond that, I have learned to lead worship through years of trial and error in my own weekly spin cycles. In God's good providence, He has allowed me the privilege of pastoring congregations filled with loving, patient people who were content to permit their pastor to learn on the job, stretching his liturgical wings in a variety of ways. This book deals with both the theory and practice of worship, but it is not a how-to book. No single book can equip a pastor to be an effective worship leader. Instead, I engage pastors in theological and liturgical reflection with the hope that they will be spurred on to think creatively about worship in their own congregational contexts.

I urge pastors to give due attention to this aspect of church life. Marva Dawn is surely correct when she says that "since worship is the only thing the church does that no one else can do, worship should be a congregation's top priority."[4] It will never be that, however, until it becomes the pastor's top priority.

At the end of the day, it will be faithful pastors who guide the church through treacherous times and enable her to flourish amid whatever cultural upheavals she may encounter. The primary vehicle for making this arduous journey will be the witness of a church unfailingly given to the worship and adoration of her Creator and Sustainer. That church's ability to so worship will be determined by the willingness of pastors to remain faithfully immersed in the weekly spin cycle of pastoral life. Yes, Sunday often comes too quickly for busy pastors. Yet the allure of what can happen on those Sundays makes this vocation the best in the world. Let those who give leadership to the worship of God's church embrace their task with vigor and with the confidence that God himself inhabits this weekly whirlwind.

—J. MICHAEL WALTERS

Pentecost 2006
Houghton, New York

## CHAPTER ONE

# CONFLICT

## *Grounding the Lightning Rod*

—⟳—

*Sometimes, worship in the church becomes a
"weapon of mass distraction."*
—Brian McClaren

### SILVER BULLET
By identifying and defusing the tensions underlying worship,
pastors free their churches to experience renewal.

*There is a balm in Gilead.* I grew up hearing those words sung by
the adults in my church. I now confess that I didn't have a clue
what they were singing. For years I labored under the impression that
they were talking about a *bomb* in Gilead. Reared in an every-time-
the-doors-are-open family, I had witnessed enough of church life that
the bomb idea made some sense. Now, after some twenty years of
pastoral ministry and more than ten years preparing people for ministry,
I'm more convinced than ever of the plausibility of a "bomb" in the
church—one designed as a weapon for use in the worship wars.

Although this war will never appear in history books, every pastor
understands that it is a real one, filled with danger, uncertainty, and
the likelihood of casualties. Nearly every congregation either has
gone or will go through some serious tension related to worship. I can

remember now, safely removed by several years, the inside joke I shared with a staff pastor during any church crisis or problem. One of us would say with a wry smile, "It could be worse; it could be a worship committee meeting." In those days nothing was less inviting than a tension-filled meeting packed with members who had strong opinions and loaded agendas. Looking back, I see that we not only survived that difficult time but also benefited from the struggles, arriving at resolutions to the issues that threatened to divide us. And those experiences have produced within me the deep conviction that nearly all pastors will deal with a host of church problems that at first glance appear to center on worship. The "bomb" is still ticking.

The good news, however, is that nearly any piece of liturgical ordnance can be defused by understanding and resolving its underlying conflict—which usually has little to do with worship itself. Worship often is a lightning rod, attracting all sorts of issues that are generated elsewhere in the life of the church. When that fact is not recognized, pastors grab for simplistic solutions that address only the presenting, not the underlying, problem. No drum kit, video projector, or professional musician can resolve the deepest conflicts that affect congregations, because those conflicts usually have nothing to do with worship, let alone with music.

Worship is the single most visible activity of any congregation. Thus it is often where the symptoms of church health show up first. But as anyone who has ever tried to cure a toothache by only relieving the pain could tell you, treating a symptom will not cure a disease. When pastors begin to view worship wars as symptoms of deeper issues, then there is hope that the ticking time bomb can be defused. Four critical issues in the life of a church have a tendency to manifest themselves in worship. They are

1. The Triumph of Culture
2. The Church's Loss of Identity
3. The Selling Out of Evangelism
4. The Pressure of Church Growth

The first step toward treating problems in the worship life of the church is to diagnose the underlying issue and deal with it. We begin with understanding the seismic shift that has taken place in our culture and seeing why it finds at its epicenter the worship of the church.

## ISSUE ONE: THE TRIUMPH OF CULTURE

I don't know exactly what went through Dorothy's mind in the first moments after she landed in the wonderful land of Oz, but she did understand that a radical change had taken place as evidenced by her famous words, "We're not in Kansas anymore." I know the feeling. As a child of the sedate church culture of the 1950s, a card-carrying member of the flower generation of the 1960s, and a seminary and graduate theological student of the 1970s and '80s, I thought I had a good grasp of the current ecclesiological landscape. Yet here in the new millennium, I find myself in a world of constant change and wondering how the church can possibly adjust. We're certainly not in the Kansas of twentieth-century church life anymore!

Yet there is no need for despair. God both ordained and sustains the church, and it will survive in some form until God brings down the curtain on human history. How the church responds (not reacts!) to the current climate of change will largely determine its immediate health and its vitality within the culture.

### THE REVERSAL OF ROLES

In postmodern culture, the claim of religious authority is automatically suspect. The day of pastors or church leaders prescriptively telling people what to think or how to behave is long gone. Today, the culture's emphasis is on the felt needs of the individual, not on objective truth. And the culture itself is less religious. The veneer of religious life that has characterized North America—especially the United States—for so long is wearing increasingly thin. Religion in general and Christianity in particular have been moved to the margins of our corporate existence, brought out for special occasions or times of national crisis but never permitted to interfere with the business of "real life." In short, the church gets no free pass from the culture these days—no automatically accorded place of respect. There is an increasingly large number of unchurched people, and unchurched Christians are one of the fastest growing segments within American Christianity.

Sociologist Alan Wolfe has written about the struggle of American churches to keep pace with the culture. As a nonbeliever himself, Wolfe provides a fascinating look at the church from the outside. Wolfe writes,

> Tracing the history of Christian thought from the New Testament to the twentieth century, the theologian H. Richard Niebuhr documented the many ways in which Christ could become a transformer of culture. But in the United States, culture has transformed Christ, as well as all other religions found within these shores. In every aspect of religious life American faith has met American culture and American culture has triumphed.[1]

This triumph of modern culture over religion has profoundly influenced the way churches operate within that culture. Because worship is the most public thing most churches do, it would be odd indeed if the church's cultural wrestling match did not manifest itself in liturgy. The problem is that the church has overreacted, conforming itself to the culture rather than responding to it. Cultural commentator Os Guinness says that the evangelical church has gone native. He writes, "For all the lofty recent statements on biblical authority, a great part of the evangelical community has made an historical shift, it has transferred authority from *sola scriptura* by scripture alone, to *sola cultura* by culture alone."[2] Even a cursory look over the ecclesiastical landscape of the twenty-first century demonstrates why Guinness and so many others are concerned.

## THE CHURCH'S REACTION

While we may well be wary of the role of culture in shaping the church, it may be argued that the church does need to change in order to address a changing world. Every church that seriously attempts to engage the culture will have to make some decision as to how it will do so. To respond thoughtlessly and unintentionally is to adopt the *sola cultura* approach. That easy alternative is the one most often taken. Steve Mullet quips, "When a church's theology holds a position of swimming upstream—and most of the church's members are floating downstream on yachts—something's got to give. Usually, it's the theology that gets sold away, not the yachts."[3] Aping the culture is a way of merely floating along on the surface. But it is inherently ineffective. Wolfe states,

> The whole idea behind this approach is that secular culture, for all its faults, knows something about getting and retaining an audience. Yet, it is not clear that the people attracted by music they already know will remain in churches to which they've been attracted. The typical praise song found in megachurches, according to a professor of preaching at Emory University, is "simplistic, repetitive, and finally, boring."[4]

This observation wonderfully summarizes why modern culture has become such a minefield for worship planners.

Perhaps at no other time in the church's history has its relationship to culture been both so crucial and so incendiary. Pastors must constantly ask what is essential to Christian worship and what is mere cultural packaging. The failure to know the difference is potentially devastating to the health of the church. But the placement of any item into either of these categories has accounted for many battles in the worship war. To what extent will the church *include* culture in order to *engage* it? That question has provoked conflict in churches all over North America as one camp has attempted to "hold back the barbarians" while the other has tried to become "seeker sensitive."

The seeker-sensitive model has become dominant, although some analysts question its staying power. Robb Redman says that the "seeker movement faces a challenge in that seeker services work well with 'nominally churched people who have been turned off in some way,' but less well with people who have no history or connection with the church."[5] Even more troubling for those churches is that backlash that tends to be created by cultural accommodation. Wolfe observes,

> Evangelicals have long found ways to reconcile their version of Christianity with the materialistic, consumption-driven American culture, whether reflected in the ostentatious lifestyles of the televangelists, the success oriented preaching of a Robert Schuller, or the explicitly pro-capitalist prosperity theology of the Kenneth Hagan ministries of Tulsa, Oklahoma. Critics have found such tendencies disturbing, not only because they seem to turn their backs on the poor and needy, but also because prosperity theology makes so few demands on those who practice it.[6]

Accommodating culture does not equate to permeating culture, and our attempts at playing ball with the dominant values of the age have often blown up in our ecclesiastical faces. That danger is especially real when dealing with the younger generation, which seeks radical authenticity and a countercultural approach to religious life.

So while the attempt to engage culture is admirable, the results have been mixed at best. Our efforts have generally lacked missional and ecclesial clarity at the denominational level, and local congregations have tended to adopt cultural trends and values for pragmatic reasons without subjecting them to critical thought. Blithely assuming that the bigger-is-better mantra that drives corporate America is likewise applicable to the church, we have too often failed to discriminate between the genuinely broad appeal of the gospel and doing "whatever it takes" to get people into the building on Sundays.

At the very forefront of the values that ought to be critically challenged is the idea that the church must embrace consumerism. The advertising industry has learned to push all the right buttons in order to generate the need to consume its products. We have adopted a similar approach in attracting congregants. Find out what the customer, er, seeker needs, then demonstrate that the church can meet that need. You need affirmation? Hey, we've got that. Child care? We've got that too. Surely, that is a short-term road to "success," fraught with dangers. Chief among them is the possibility that we will enthrone the desires of the consumer in the place of a holy God.

## THE NEED TO ENGAGE

Allowing the culture to dictate the church's responses and actions is a recipe for disaster. The kingdom of God seeks to transform that culture, not be molded by it. Being culturally sensitive is necessary and wise, but to allow the producers of reality TV, pop fiction, and talk radio to determine how the church should worship is to wave the white flag of surrender in the worship war. The kingdom of God and the kingdom of this world are simply incompatible in some areas. To lead worship effectively and authentically, pastors must know which things are negotiable and which are not.

This does not mean, however, that the church should turn its back on the culture. That, too, would be a colossal failure. Finding ways to engage the culture with biblical and theological integrity is the crying need of our day. Happily, there are encouraging signs of the emergence of new alternatives in engaging the culture Christianly. Emerging worship, sometimes ironically called *ancient-future faith*, is a movement that contends that it is possible for Christians to engage the culture without giving in to it. The church need not roll over for the culture, but neither does the church need to be at war with it. There are biblically informed, creative ways to dialogue with the culture, and the future of ministry in the West is largely tied to that dialogue. The key to engaging in that dialogue with integrity is to begin with a clear understanding of what the church is and what is its role in the world, a role that is most vividly expressed in worship. And that brings us to the second critical issue that underlies the worship wars: the church's own loss of self-identity.

## ISSUE TWO: THE CHURCH'S LOSS OF IDENTITY

"Regardless of where one begins, one always comes back to the church." Those are the words of Cardinal Joseph Ratzinger, now known to the world as Pope Benedict XVI. The pope is right about this much: Ecclesiology is fundamentally important for everything we do. Many of the issues pastors face as worship wars are rooted in our failure to hold to a sound doctrine of the church. Foundational to disarming the worship wars in any local congregation is for pastors to grasp that much of the current tension about worship results from uncertainty regarding the church's role or mission in the world. This critical lack of self-identity is nowhere more clearly seen than in our constant pursuit of our culture's most cherished value—relevance.

### THE MYTH OF RELEVANCE

The combination of panic at dwindling numbers, angst over the exodus of our youth from the church, and the church's increasing marginalization in the culture has produced a Chicken Little–like mentality that has caused the church to fall prey to every gimmick and quick fix that has come down the pike—and the traffic has been bumper to bumper for a while now!

The church's struggle to find some way to justify its continued existence in a culture that is completely disinterested in it has led some to adopt *relevance* as their primary mission. But Os Guinness is right to ask the obvious question: "Relevance for what, relevant to whom?"[7] The church doesn't have the luxury of relating itself only to the culture; it must relate itself to Christ. We are, after all, His body. The life and teachings of Jesus are the chart and compass for how the church navigates within the world. Nothing could be more relevant to

22

this culture or any other. I've never heard anyone take a fair-minded look at Christ's teachings, His valuing of human beings, truth, justice, and reconciliation and then contend that Jesus is irrelevant.

The church must regain its confidence in the power of the gospel to be relevant to every time and place. If it does not, it will continue to chase after the affirmation of a world that, frankly, sees the church as unnecessary. Our attempts to prove our worth to the culture will eventually have just the opposite effect—we will be further marginalized and ignored. Worse, we will lose what is left of our mission and moral authority as we constantly ask the forlorn question "Why doesn't anybody like me?" The remedy for the church in this age is not to focus on its relationship to the world but to reassert its relationship to Christ. We must regain our grasp of and commitment to our own scriptural identity as the people of God in the world. God's people have always been a pilgrim people, refugees if you will. The church's calling is not to settle down with the citizens of the world but to live out the faith in a way that will cause others to ask, "What must I do to be saved?"

## THE NEED FOR INCARNATION

Some congregations have reinvented themselves in creative ways that are faithful to the church's calling, while others have staggered from one ecclesiastical fad to the next like drunken sailors. The difference between the two is the possession of an ecclesiological vision that is strong enough to engage the culture without being subverted by it. In terms of worship, this involves the creative employment of those aspects of culture that truly serve the church's interests. Like missionaries, we pastors must contextualize our message so that it will be intelligible to those around us. But this is a far cry from uncritically borrowing cultural fads in a vain effort to keep oneself on the cutting edge or culturally relevant. "How we engage the popular culture should reflect our core theological beliefs and avoid the extreme of taking our cultural surroundings either too seriously, or not seriously enough."[8] Methodist theologian Tex Sample points to the deeper concern that we face. "The issue," he says, "is not relevance . . . The issue is incarnation. When so-called traditional churches are out of touch with the people who live around them, the problem is not that they are irrelevant but that they are not incarnational."[9]

That the church is Christ's body in the world is the most basic tenet of ecclesiology. If a local church fails to engage the culture around it in redemptive, transformational ways, that church fails not only to be relevant but also to be authentically the church. Rather than convincing the world of how relevant it is, the church should be finding ways to help the world become relevant to what God is doing in the world through the church. Instead of either avoiding the popular altogether or embracing it completely, the church must critically adapt cultural forms that serve its missional purpose in the world.

Becoming truly incarnational clearly involves more than what happens in worship. Much of the current tension in worship results from our attempts to use worship alone to fulfill the church's mission. That cannot be done, though many fine pastors will die trying. Yet how the church worships can help to demonstrate to the world what the church is truly about. Marva Dawn contends,

> If the church's worship is faithful, it will eventually be subversive of the culture surrounding it, for God's truth transforms the lives of those nurtured by it. Worship will turn our values, habits, and ideas upside down as it forms our character; only then will we be genuinely right side up eternally. Only then will we know a joy worthy of our destiny.[10]

Worship has transformative power, and a congregation that rightly worships God will sooner of later be a leavening influence in its community.

## THE NEED FOR COMMON LIFE

When the church embraces its true mission, it will display values that are exactly opposite of the world's. As I think about the values Jesus championed in His own life and taught as elements of the kingdom of God, those that stand out are the idea of welcoming the stranger and treating one another as neighbors. These are the values that are so often sacrificed on the worship battlefields of the church. As Don Saliers says, "At the root of so much of our so-called 'problem with worship' and the various debates currently raging between the 'traditional' and 'contemporary' styles, is the lack of sustained common life."[11] Where there is no connection between what we do outside the sanctuary and inside it, there will be conflict over worship. Our worship wars are merely a symptom of our failure in another aspect of the church's life—fellowship.

Far too many churches are trying to encapsulate their entire communal life into one hour on Sunday morning. It is impossible to live out the life of the church in a worship service alone, particularly if the worship of God—the vertical axis—is our primary focus during that hour. Church members who participate only in the worship of the church are very likely to feel that their "needs" are not being met, because worship is not about our needs but about God. Therefore, much of the stress congregations experience over worship can be attributed to their nominal commitment to Christ and to each other.

This explains also why worship wars are an exclusively Western phenomenon. Churches that argue over worship do so because they have too much time on their hands, often because they are not occupied with fulfilling the church's mission. Can you imagine the persecuted church in various parts of the world wasting its time on criticizing the pastor's communication techniques or the style of music selected? Few things could be more unseemly than for Christian brothers and sisters to fight with, avoid, and censure one another over the adoration of God. If the singing of *my* music has become more important to me than the love of my brothers and sisters, I have something much more serious than a worship problem. I have a basic misunderstanding of the Christian faith. It is possible that most congregations that are fighting over worship need to "get a life"—a common life as the body of Christ.

If one of the underlying factors in the worship war is that the church has lost its focus, then one of the remedies will be for pastors to preach more often about the doctrine of the church and to do so unapologetically. Enabling our congregations to understand who we are and what we have been called to do in the world may be the most effective of all worship techniques.

## ISSUE THREE: THE SELLING OUT OF EVANGELISM

The modern church has chosen to respond to culture primarily by accommodation. Its approach has been to attract people to the church by appealing to some felt need, primarily the need to belong. The worship service has been the primary venue for this cultural engagement. Yet there is a deeper issue here than the subjugation of worship to cultural relevance—troubling though that is. The warring that takes place over the conduct of worship is a symbol of the modern church's ambivalence toward and confusion about evangelism.

### THE OLD SCHOOL: THE EVANGELISTIC SERVICE

In the revivalistic tradition in which I was raised, there were three primary church services held each week. There was a midweek prayer meeting, usually held on Wednesday evening. There was the Sunday morning worship service, of course, always preceded by a Sunday school hour. And there was the Sunday evening service, which was typically referred to as the evangelistic service. Sunday morning was devoted to worship and a sermon aimed at an audience of believers. But Sunday evening was a different story. The Sunday evening service was overtly evangelistic, and the sermons—often a good hellfire-and-brimstone oration, packed with stories about unrepentant sinners dying on their way home from church—always culminated in an altar call.

In the early 1970s, churches like mine noticed that there were few or no unconverted folk attending these Sunday evening services. Pastors began to use Sunday morning services—which were more often attended by nonbelievers—for evangelism and to reserve their preaching "to the church" for Sunday evening. The switch was on.

Today, churches that hold Sunday evening services are rare, and few or none of them use the time for evangelism. This has left the average church with one primary service and, given our current understanding of the nature of evangelism, only one occasion each week in which to evangelize the lost. Evangelism is now done primarily in the church building, during the primary service, by the pastor and his or her leadership team.

## THE NEW WAVE: SEEKER-SENSITIVE WORSHIP

This current style of evangelism, not surprisingly, has had a tremendous impact on worship. Churches are more and more concerned that their primary service be accessible to nonbelievers, usually referred to as *seekers*. Seeker sensitivity is the primary aim of worship in many churches and is a concern for nearly all congregations.

It is true that all worship should be seeker sensitive in that all worshipers are seekers after God—or should be. Yet worship and evangelism are not the same thing, and both have suffered to some degree by their association. The Willow Creek Community in the Chicago area has been the most visibly successful congregation to employ the seeker-sensitive approach and is often used as the model for this method. Seeker sensitive worship itself is often referred to as the Willow Creek approach. I have attended there and read much of their literature, and this congregation is largely successful at maintaining a distinction between worship and evangelism. They clearly talk about the need for believers to be present in what they call new community services on week nights, which are structured for believers and emphasize a God-focused approach to worship.

This distinction, however, is not always maintained by others who have adopted the seeker sensitive approach to evangelism. Constructing a church service designed primarily to appeal to people who "don't do church" relegates evangelism to an institutional model that probably cannot be sustained in our increasingly unchurched—even antichurch—culture. The real problem with "unchurched Harry and Mary," after all, is not that they don't like church but that they don't know God. Most congregations that have adopted the seeker model do not offer the equivalent of Willow Creek's New Community service, a gathering aimed at leading the believing community in worship. In many congregations where the entire focus of Sunday morning is evangelism, there is a steady stream of malnourished believers exiting through the back door. Marva Dawn describes the difference between worship and evangelism in this way:

> Worship is the language of love and growth between believers and God. Evangelism is the language of introduction between those who believe and those who don't. To confuse the two, and put on worship the burden of evangelism robs the people of God of their responsibility to care about the neighbor, defrauds the believer of transforming depth, and steals from God the profound praise of which He is worthy.[12]

## THE BETTER MODEL: EVANGELISM BY ALL

One of the primary stresses in modern church ministry results from the expectation that the pastor or ordained clergy be the primary evangelists in the church. Evangelism, which should be the responsibility of *all* Christians, has been subtly placed back into the lap of the pastor. Congregation members see their role in the process as inviting their unchurched friends to a worship service. After that, it is up to the pastor to create an experience that sufficiently interests the newcomers. The confusion of worship and evangelism has adversely affected both activities and added stress to the already pressure-packed vocation of the clergy. Until Christians learn to accept the role of all believers in sharing their faith and helping to bring others to God, the worship wars will likely continue as pastors and congregations disagree over both the purpose of the church's main gathering and the responsibility for conducting evangelism.

All this is not to say that genuine worship is not evangelistic. I had an amazing conversation with a student a few years ago who told me that he came to know Christ one Sunday morning while standing in the balcony of our church, participating in a responsive reading from the Old Testament. I believe that when God is properly adored and praised, His Spirit will powerfully draw people to himself. Evangelism, in this case, was not the primary aim of the service; it resulted because someone who was truly seeking God was placed in a setting where God was honored and chose to reveal himself. This happens often in worship, but that result is much different than our attempts to "put on a good show" for nonbelievers. Both worship and evangelism are far too important to allow that to happen.

## ISSUE FOUR: THE PRESSURE FOR CHURCH GROWTH

The first salvo in a local church's worship war is often fired as the congregation's attempts to reinvent itself in response to declining attendance. Our culture is enamored with statistics, and churches are continually asked to quantify their success. Every pastor knows that when it comes to evaluating the church, it is much easier to count people than to evaluate the condition of their hearts. So we count. And when the number is down, everyone feels the pressure to reverse the trend.

Usually, the first place leaders look to boost attendance is the church's worship style, and that may be the prelude to a worship war. Pastors easily get caught in the crossfire between those arguing for more substance in worship and those arguing for changes in the style of worship. Often it is a false dilemma. The idea that a congregation must choose between worship that is substantive and worship that appeals to people is simply false. Constructing worship that is both theologically sound *and* culturally sensitive is not easy and will most likely require a good bit of training of the congregation. But the result is worth the effort because it provides a means of defusing the "bomb in Gilead."

Also, thoughtful, God-centered worship is more likely to succeed in attracting congregants than is a consumer-centered approach. Marva Dawn is right in saying that "the greatest danger for the marketing approach to sharing the gospel with the world around the church is that it treats people as consumers—perhaps religious consumers, but consumers nonetheless."[13] The generation that most desperately needs the attention of the church is a generation that does not respond positively to a consumeristic approach to the faith. These are people longing to encounter something transcendent, authentic, even mysterious. We have good news for them. We need not back away from the truth of the gospel: It is the enduring good news. And wherever that gospel is truly preached and is incarnated in worship, people will be powerfully drawn to the Savior.

No one ever leaves a church because its worship is too meaningful. But people often leave because the worship is too shallow. To further dilute worship in order to gain an audience is futile. As worship leaders, we can be creative and innovative, taking the culture into full account. Yet we must remember that while we "don't put new wine into worn out skins . . . that new wine necessarily comes from old juice."[14] Pastors, take your people deep with God, and you will discover the single most effective way to keep peace in the church.

## GROUNDING THE LIGHTNING ROD

Worship is a lightning rod, attracting energy from all quarters of the church. Congregational problems gravitate toward worship with incredible speed and force. Pastors must be able to sense the deeper issues that are often present during a worship war and realize that "fixing" the problem won't necessarily bring peace to the church. In any case, worship is not a problem to be solved but an ongoing relationship to be cultivated between God and His people. And as with all relationships, what it needs most is the dedicated time and attention of the parties involved. Paying attention to the worship of the church, being aware of what's happening or not happening, is the first order of business. Absolute agreement about worship within a congregation is unlikely this side of heaven, but mature congregations that have a clear sense of mission can at least agree on the importance of worshiping together with integrity. Far too often, the worship life of a church is addressed only when necessary to solve a problem or attract newcomers. Yet worship is a full-time concern of the church and should be an ongoing interest for both pastor and people. Perhaps when we become more concerned with spiritual depth of our churches than with their size, or with the holiness of God than with the scope of our influence, there will be less debate among us and more authentic seeking after God.

If I could ask only one question about a church that was calling me as its pastor, it would be this one: What happens when you come together on Sunday morning? Understanding that aspect of the church's life would tell me more about it than anything else. Worship is the engine that drives a healthy church, and tending it well should be a front-burner concern for every pastor. Many current problems we know as the worship wars have resulted from our neglect of worship more so than from our failure to adequately address the culture. Too many of us have fallen asleep at the wheel.

Leading worship in a local church can be a bit like fielding a bouncing football. There are too many possibilities, and it always seems to bounce in the wrong direction. But the alternative to taking on this challenge is to surrender the church's most vulnerable area to the culture. And remember that we are not alone in this task. No pastor should feel as if the future of the church's worship rests on his or her shoulders alone. Worship was God's idea, not ours. And while culture is a powerful force and can be an imposing adversary to the church's mission, it is not all powerful. The balm in Gilead is real. Pastors can give themselves to the hard work of worship knowing that they have entered a partnership with the God who has issued this cosmic call to worship. As we leaders allow the healing balm to bring peace to our own lives, we will find the confidence and creativity to offer God's peace to a world in which the "war" over worship is the very least problem.

## CHAPTER TWO

# FOUNDATIONS

## *Why Worship Matters*

—⟋⟍⟍—

*So how do we manage to live believingly and obediently
in and under this revealed sovereignty in a world that is
mostly either ignorant or defiant of it? Worship shaped
by an obedient reading of Scripture is basic. We submit
to having our imaginations and behaviors conditioned
by the reality of God rather than by what is handed
out in school curricula and media reporting.*

—Eugene Peterson

### SILVER BULLET
Planning worship is the first priority for
creating a vibrant congregation.

Picture, if you will, a typical Sunday morning worship service. Children fidget in their seats while their parents alternately try to restrain them and join them in daydreaming more diverting pursuits. A minimally prepared choir awkwardly navigates the weekly anthem, sharps and flats blending somehow into a passable offering. Bored teenagers are clustered in the back two rows, turning every few moments to see if the clock on the rear wall is still working—and wondering why the preacher can't see it. As the service ends, the congregation lifts its voice in song, pledging to love God and serve others. Finally, it is over.

What just happened?

That scene, played ten thousand times each Sunday, typifies the worship experience in an average church. Do the participants understand what they've done or why it matters? Do you? What is it, exactly, that God desires in these weekly gatherings of ours? And why does He desire it? That God desires our worship is abundantly clear from Scripture. But why?

I've been asked that question countless times in the classroom. "Why does God ask us to worship Him? How does it benefit Him?" What they are really asking is this: Why does worship matter? Unlike some questions, which are easily disposed of or deflected, this question is of fundamental importance. It is a question that demands an answer. Why, indeed, do we do what we do on Sunday mornings? Why do we worship?

Most pastors, I believe, understand that worship is important. What's less clear to many of us is *why* it matters. We know, for example, that the Sunday worship service is what James White calls the congregation's front door to the wider community.[1] We feel a sense of urgency to make the worship service the world's entry portal into the kingdom of heaven. We know that this hour matters — but we have perhaps the wrong reason in mind. Robert Webber, who has done as much as anyone in the evangelical church for worship renewal, summarizes the situation this way:

> Evangelicals are familiar with this story. But for the most part, evangelicals seem to be unaware that this story lies at the heart of worship. Evangelicals generally have defined worship in one of two ways, neither of which grasps the biblical imperative of worship.
>
> The first sees worship as ascribing worth to God. In this half-truth definition the burden of worship is placed upon the worshiping community. The community of worship, it seems, must originate words and feelings of praise through music and prayer that God will find pleasing.

The second is a presentational approach to worship. Here worship consists of a series of packaged presentations to the "audience," so that they may hear the message. The error of both forms of worship is that they do not recognize the Divine side of worship.[2]

Worship itself, to say nothing of its impact upon church health, is far too important to be left to either liturgical preferences or cultural whims. Nothing indicates the health of a church any more accurately than the worship life of the people. C. S. Lewis said that "praise almost seems to be inner health made audible."[3] Surely, the worship of a people is a commentary on their hearts. Understanding why worship plays such a critical role in church health takes us necessarily first to Scripture, then to a consideration of some theological assumptions and affirmations, and finally to a review of the mission of the church in the world.

## WORSHIP IN SCRIPTURE

By observing how those in Scripture worshiped, we can begin to formulate an answer to the question of why worship matters. And we can apply those observations to our own attempts to worship authentically. Once we understand *why* worship matters, we can begin to know *how* it should be done. Looking at the biblical foundations of worship will reveal why so many of our quick-fix approaches are doomed to fail. We'll come to see that we are not free to invent what worship is or how, broadly speaking, it should be done. We have a framework for understanding worship, and that is Scripture.

## THE FAILURE TO WORSHIP IS SIN

Worship matters, first, because the failure to worship is the essence of sin. Scripture is filled with exhortations to worship God. Much might be gained from examining the biblical calls to worship, but perhaps it will better suit our purpose to look at a worship-related passage that is a bit darker in its treatment of the subject:

The wrath of God is being revealed from heaven against all the godlessness and wickedness of men who suppress the truth by their wickedness, since what may be known about God is plain to them, because God has made it plain to them. For since the creation of the world God's invisible qualities—his eternal power and divine nature—have been clearly seen, being understood from what has been made, so that men are without excuse. For although they knew God, they neither glorified him as God nor gave thanks to him, but their thinking became futile and their foolish hearts were darkened. Although they claimed to be wise, they became fools and exchanged the glory of the immortal God for images made to look like mortal man and birds and animals and reptiles. Therefore, God gave them over in the sinful desires of their hearts to sexual impurity for the degrading of their bodies with one another. They exchanged the truth of God for a lie, and worshiped and served created things rather than the Creator—who is forever praised. Amen (Rom. 1:18–25).

The apostle Paul here gives what some have termed a theological account of the Fall. Whereas the account in Genesis 3 offers a narrative version of humankind's choice to sin, in Romans 1 Paul is more interested in the fact that this choice resulted in God's wrath being directed against His creation. One is immediately struck by the refusal of human beings to submit to God's authority, to confess His worthiness, or to honor His majesty. In short, this is a failure to worship. The result of this catastrophic failure to acknowledge God as God is that human "worship" devolved into veneration of created things along with the wholesale perversion of human life that may be expected when truth is exchanged for a lie. The whole sordid history of human sinfulness, as Paul saw it, began as a failure to worship. Don Saliers wrote that sin might be regarded as "transubstantiating in reverse—turning God's glory into something pedestrian."[4] The apostle Paul would likely agree.

Any pastor who tires of ordering the Sunday service and sadly concludes, "Oh well, it's good enough," would do well to recall the chilling reminder of Romans 1. Worship matters! It is the means by which we express our humanity—our status as created beings—in the most truthful of ways. Thomas Long observes that "authentic worship genuinely meets people's needs because people need to worship. Worshiping God is not simply a good thing to do, it is necessary, it is a necessary thing to do to be human."[5]

Worship is never very far from the surface or intent of any biblical text. From the story of Creation, which some have termed a cosmic call to worship, to the indescribable scenes of the Apocalypse, the praise of God is of foremost interest in Scripture. It has been said that Abel was the first victim of the worship wars. While that may stretch the point a bit, there is no ignoring the fact that God takes worship most seriously. So should we.

## GOD INITIATES WORSHIP

Worship is important also because it is an activity that God initiates with His creation in order to maintain a relationship with them. According to the Oxford English Dictionary, "to worship is to honor or revere the supernatural being or power or the holy thing; to regard or approach with veneration; to adore with appropriate acts or ceremonies."[6] But prior to this action, appropriate as it is, must come the redemptive initiative of God. Acceptable worship never begins with human intuition or inventiveness but with divine action. Worship is a response.[7]

The story of Israel and its covenant relationship with God is a narrative of worship. God gives His law to the people of Israel as their means of establishing and maintaining a relationship with Him. The word that most accurately captures the manner in which that relationship is sustained is *worship*. The fact that God regarded some worship in the Old Testament as unacceptable is a reminder that what seems to be impressive or appropriate by human understanding may be deeply offensive to God. Peterson notes that "acceptable worship under both covenants is a matter of responding to God's initiative in salvation and revelation and doing so in a way that He requires."[8] God sent prophets to call a wayward people back to himself, and, more often than not, the prophetic critique centered in the area of worship. Israel's stern judgment at the hand of God in both the eighth and sixth centuries before Christ resulted primarily from the failure of its covenantal relationship with God, which was demonstrated first and foremost in worship. Although worship could be expressed in a number of ways by the Israelites, it was the attitude of the heart that really mattered.[9] Acceptable worship in the Old Testament included homage, service, and reverence, demonstrated in the whole of life. We worship as a way of keeping ourselves in harmony with God.

## WORSHIP MAINTAINS OUR RELATIONSHIP WITH GOD

A third reason worship is vitally important is that it brings us into intimacy with God. Authentic worship always brings us face-to-face with our sinful condition. As Isaiah discovered, a worship experience that reveals the holiness of God will simultaneously reveal our own sinfulness. The result will be confession. (See Isa. 6.) To be in God's presence is to see ourselves for what we truly are.

Yet our modern services routinely ignore or gloss over this aspect of worship. We avoid seeing God as He truly is because we wish to avoid seeing ourselves as we truly are. As a result, we miss the opportunity to receive God's gracious invitation to experience forgiveness.

Our modern attempt to avoid "sin talk" effectively turns the truth of God into a lie, completely undermining the true intent of worship.

The New Testament continues these themes, albeit on a more focused level, centered on the person and work of Jesus Christ. Jesus is the very incarnation of God, but He is not recognized as God (Rom. 1:18) and is not counted worthy of worship except by those who submit to Him. The story of Jesus' life, death, and resurrection forms the basis for the church to be called, as a new covenant people, into a relationship with the Creator. Jesus is the new Exodus, the ultimate saving event of God. He thus becomes the new center of worship for people of faith.

Beyond this, the New Testament hints at the role of the Trinity in authentic worship. Peterson notes that "through the ministry of the Son and the Spirit, the Father obtains true worshipers, thus the doctrine of the Trinity lies at the heart of a truly Christian theology of worship. Each Person of the Godhead plays a significant role in establishing the worship appropriate to the new covenant era."[10] Observing the worship of many evangelical churches, it would be difficult to determine whether the Trinity was a tenet of the church's doctrine. Happily, several contemporary evangelical worship leaders are beginning to recover the place of the Trinity in worship by composing music and litanies with Trinitarian themes and by finding creative ways to honor Father, Son, and Holy Spirit in corporate worship. This is an important step toward taking the New Testament seriously.

## WORSHIP BUILDS COMMUNITY

The New Testament has much less to say about the manner in which worship should be done than does the Old Testament. While the New Testament is clear about the central focus of worship—Jesus Christ—it is less clear about how worship should be conducted. Most modern liturgical scholars agree that the search to discover an authentically New Testament style of worship is pointless, because worship practices tended to evolve according to local customs and needs. So no church can honestly claim to have *the* New Testament model for worship practices. Even in the early church, there seems to have been a variety of worship styles and practices in use. Yet there is one unmistakable worship emphasis recorded in the pages of the New Testament, and it should catch the attention of every modern-day worship leader. That emphasis is *community*.

The early church functioned corporately, not individually. It was an assembly, a gathering of believers. Preserving this emphasis on community is one function of the doctrine of the Trinity. Also, the concern for corporate well-being (and not merely individual growth) colors everything we know about worship in the New Testament. For example, apart from the church's concern for community, it is impossible to completely grasp Paul's admonitions about worship and spiritual gifts in 1 Corinthians 12–14. Paul's insistence upon the edification of the church is an important component in a biblical theology of worship. Peterson writes that "In contemporary English, to say that something was 'edifying,' usually means that it was personally helpful or encouraging. But it is easy to misinterpret Paul and to think of edification individualistically meaning the spiritual advancement of individuals within the church. This term, however, regularly has a corporate reference in the Apostle's teaching."[11] So the real question in evaluating the effectiveness of worship is not "Did I enjoy that?" but "Did that build up the church?" Peterson goes on to note that while most people say they go to church to "worship God," the primary purpose of Christian assembly is the edification of the church. We accomplish that, in part, through worship.[12] That seemingly minor distinction has great ramifications for worship. In our consumerist culture, the challenge for worship leaders is to help parishioners understand that going to church is necessarily different than going to Wal-Mart. Joining the corporate worship of the body of Christ requires that we allow something else—the good of the body—to supercede our personal preferences.

## WORSHIP IS OUR RESPONSE TO GOD

We've noted that worship is initiated by God. It is our response to God for His acts of grace. In the Old Testament, the Exodus stands as the central event in the worship of Israel; in the New Testament, the Christ event is central. In both cases God has acted redemptively on behalf of His people. Worship is a response to that redemptive and loving initiative. That's one reason prayer is central to worship. It is our most direct way of expressing our thanks and praise to God for what He has done. Robert Webber writes that the Bible seems to suggest four essential kinds of worship responses.[13]

*Remember.* First, the people remember. When God's people gather for worship they are remembering what He has done for them. But this remembering is more than simply recalling some event in far-off history. The word used in Scripture is the Greek word *anamnesis*, which is not merely to remember but to recall the event in a way that makes it personal. This is the kind of "remembering" Moses exhorted the people of Israel to engage in once they entered the Promised Land. The feasts of Israel were intended to help the people recall God's savings acts in a way that would continue to shape their lives. This type of recollection lies behind those words of Jesus, so often inscribed on our communion tables: "Do this in remembrance of Me." We remember the death of Christ so that it may have an effect upon us.

*Anticipate.* In the Bible, the response of the people in worship is anticipatory. Biblical worship looks both to the past and the future. This is why we necessarily speak of the eschatological character of worship. To celebrate the Lord's Supper, for example, is to anticipate that day when the redeemed church, as the bride of Christ, will sit down at the marriage supper. Worship always looks ahead.

*Celebrate.* Third, people at worship are always in celebration. The word *celebration* is grossly overused today. But biblical worship calls us to truly celebrate God's redemptive acts through feasting, song, and praise. Worship as celebration does not preclude confession or lament. It simply recognizes God's saving initiatives for what they are—gifts.

*Serve.* Finally, worship is a call to serve. "Enter to worship, depart to serve." That motto may seem cliché, but it is true. One of the most common complaints leveled by the Old Testament prophets against the worship of Israel was that Israel had forgotten the horizontal dimension of worship. To lavish praise on the Creator and then ignore or despise His creatures makes worship inauthentic.

Why is worship important? Scripture shows that worship is important because it binds us to God and to each other as believers. God calls us to worship repeatedly, and that worship leads us into deeper relationship with Him and with the church.

## THEOLOGICAL REFLECTIONS ON WORSHIP

The question "Why does worship matter?" goes to the very heart of the human situation in the world. Digging deeper into that question will provide the understanding needed to guide the church's worship in these tension-filled times. But this will call for theological reflection. How does theology answer the question "Why worship?"

### WORSHIP CORRECTS OUR INWARD FOCUS

First, let's adjust the question so often posed by students in my classroom: "What does God benefit from our worship?" He gains nothing. The real question is what does worship do for us? Roman Catholic scholar James Alison wrote, "It is entirely for our benefit that we are commanded to worship God, because if we don't we will have no protection at all against the other sort of worship. We will allow our hearts to be formed by the desires of the contradictory social other that is around us, and that heart will eventually participate in its own heartbreak and self-destruction."[14] So that's it. We worship to protect ourselves *from ourselves!* As Alison says, "true worship is lifelong therapy for distorted desire."

Augustine and Luther described the human condition following the Fall as *incurvatus in se*, curved back upon itself. It is our fallen nature to turn away from the Creator and toward ourselves with disastrous results. Worship is a form of therapy for that condition because it involves an authentic seeking after God and not oneself. Worship is a test of our willingness to forsake self and turn, in gratitude and adoration, to God. And because to lose oneself is to find oneself, the act of worship is supremely transforming. To worship God is to retrain human desire upon its intended focus—the Creator. The product of such retraining is what the Bible calls a saint, a holy person, one set apart for God and His purposes. That is the transforming potential of worship and something every pastor wants to see in his or her congregation.

## WORSHIP CONNECTS US WITH REALITY

Beyond the immediate effect of righting our view of ourselves, worship enables us to see how we are perceived by God. I recall hearing William Willimon, formerly dean of the chapel at Duke University, tell of speaking at an inner-city church that comprised mostly minorities. Willimon said, "I didn't get up to speak until almost two hours into the service!" Afterward, Willimon questioned the pastor about the length of the service, which was much greater than that in a typical suburban church. The response of this minority pastor to a white clergyman was telling. The pastor said,

> Unemployment runs nearly 50 percent here. For our youth, the unemployment rate is much higher. That means that, when our people go about during the week, everything they see, everything they hear tells them, "You are a failure. You are nobody" . . . I get them together, here in the church and through the hymns, the prayers, the preaching say, "That's a lie. You are somebody. You are royalty!" . . . It takes me so long to get them straight because the world perverts them so terribly.

One distorted desire worship therapeutically heals is the desire to believe the lie of our culture that declares human beings to be socioeconomic units rather than objects of God's love. Worship is reality therapy. To truly worship God is to align ourselves with the truth about God, self, and the world. To enable people to do that makes all those Saturday-night anxieties eminently worth the trouble. Any pastor who has ever seen the flash of recognition in the eyes of someone who finally gets it, who finally grasps the fact that God values him beyond anything he could imagine, has been paid more handsomely than any Wall Street banker. Worship changes the way we see ourselves, the way we see God, and the way we interpret the world. Worship changes us.

So then, the answer to our question "Why does God want us to praise Him?" lies in God's redemptive intention for His creation. God doesn't need our praise. But when we acknowledge Him, His glory, majesty, and sovereign rule over all—in other words, when we worship—we truly realize the purpose of our creation. We find ourselves in Him. This makes worship supremely significant to the church and thus to the pastor who leads it. Keeping this purpose before us enables us to sort through trappings that currently attend our worship. While they may make for an attractive package, they may also hide the treasure within—the reconnection of people with God and with His purpose for themselves.

## EVALUATING WORSHIP

Knowing why worship matters sheds a great deal of light on what many people see as the most pressing worship question: How? Having gained an understanding of why worship is so vitally important in the lives of believers and for the church, we now have a lens through which to examine the practice of worship. Liturgical scholar James White helpfully suggests three norms for evaluating Christian worship according to the purposes we have uncovered by Scripture and theological reflection. They are theological, historical, and pastoral.[15] To those I would add a fourth norm: missiological.

### THEOLOGICAL NORMS

The theological norm asks the question "What does our worship say about God?" Indeed, if we were to objectively examine our worship, would we conclude that God was a North American or that He was a God who loves the whole world? Does our worship have meaning only within the walls of the church? What does God expect from us in worship? These are the kinds of theological questions pastors have to ask of the church's worship. Evaluating worship according to the theological norm is not a vague, academic exercise. It ensures that worship maintains its intended focus.

## HISTORICAL NORMS

Historical norms keep us connected to the vital tradition of the faith. Note that *tradition* is singular. To be historically rooted to the faith is not to be slavishly handcuffed to old methods and outdated liturgies. Churches should find new ways of saying and doing things in worship, but those new forms should be clearly recognizable as Christian and should not simply mimic the trends of pop culture. One of the most exciting developments in modern worship is the "back to the future" movement in which ancient liturgical practices are being reinvented for today's believing communities. Willimon reminds us that "one of the best ways to arrive where we want to be today in worship is to first know where the church's worship has been before.[16]

## PASTORAL NORMS

The pastoral norm examines the accessibility of worship to the people. This is at once the most obvious and most easily abused criterion for evaluating worship. Of course worship must be both directed toward God and meaningful to people. To make it so is not easy, however, and on many Sundays we will likely be off balance in one direction or the other. The good news is that we get another opportunity next week. The even better news is that our people really do want to meaningfully worship God and are likely to be forgiving of our missteps as worship leaders if they sense that we are honestly trying to lead them on that journey. Worship is not an exercise in perfection; it includes much trial and error. It helps if we know that and especially if our people know that. Our pastoral critiques of worship ought always to reflect the grace and love of the Father toward our well-intentioned efforts.

## MISSIOLOGICAL NORMS

The most important norm we apply to worship has to do with the role worship plays in the church itself. To pastorally assess worship leads us inevitably to consider the church's mission in the world. Jesus portrayed the kingdom of God as a sphere of authority through which the purposes of God could be realized in the world. So the church is a means to a godly end. So the practical questions of worship—place, method, music, and the like—are really missiological questions. This is not to say that worship is utilitarian, useful only as a means to some end. Yet the church's worship functions in the life of the church similarly to the way it functions in the life of an individual. So just as worship will turn a self-centered heart toward God, it will also turn a self-centered church toward the world—and thereby turn a self-centered world toward God. We will fully appreciate the significance of the church's worship and the rationale behind liturgical acts only when we clearly see the church's mission in the world.

The authenticity of churches has traditionally been evaluated by classic marks including preaching of the Word, the offering of sacraments, and practicing discipline. Nowadays churches tend to be evaluated by the size of their congregations and the quality of their programs. But what if churches were evaluated primarily by the effect they have on the culture around them? How might the structure of our worship change if it were designed to help the church fulfill its mission rather than to satisfy a consumer demand? Historian Christopher Dawson contends that a society's cult—that is, what it worships—is the root of its culture. A healthy cult will produce a strong culture. Conversely, the existence of an unhealthy culture indicates a weak cult. If that is true, there is little reason to celebrate the strength of the church in North America. It would be difficult indeed to argue that the cult (Christian worship, in this case) is having any beneficial effect upon the culture. In fact there are sobering indications that modern worship is derived from the surrounding culture rather than driving it. If we are to worship authentically, according to the purposes discovered in Scripture, then we must honestly assess the state of the church and its worship by missiological norms. Do we shape the world, or are we shaped by it?

## THE NEXT GENERATION

Worship matters. It is commanded by God not for His benefit but for ours—as individuals and as a church. It connects us with God, forms us into a community, and empowers us to change the world. For this reason, pastors dare not fall asleep at the wheel as worship planners. Beyond that, we must seize the opportunity for shaping the culture of both our congregations and the world around us through worship.

How is culture transmitted from one generation to the next? In the Walters family, that was done through holiday dinners and family reunions. Through these gatherings, relatives who were barely known to us became fast friends. Adults would look at photo albums and retell childhood stories—the meta-narrative of our family. And like all families, we would eat. The family that eats together really does stay together. And the church that worships together likewise binds itself together. At the very heart of the Christian faith is the profoundly held conviction that we are a historical people, a story-formed people, as Stanley Hauerwas puts it, whose roots are to be found in the stories of Israel, in the life and teachings of Jesus, and in the struggles of the early Christian community as recorded in the pages of the New Testament.[17] And when we share our family meal—the Eucharist—we who barely knew one another become bonded as friends, brothers, sisters. What does God gain from our praise? Nothing, beyond the joy He must experience at seeing His creation in step with His loving intent. It is what we gain that makes worship the most important thing that a congregation can do.

## CHAPTER THREE

# CURRENTS

## *Why Worship Isn't Easy*

—⟋⟍—

*Church is where people go to make their*
*last stand against God.*
—Karl Barth

### SILVER BULLET
Worship planners must resist cultural forces to
keep worship focused on God.

You'd think it would be easy. Human beings are, after all, created for worship. We are made in the image of God, designed for intimate fellowship with the Father. Worship should come naturally to members of the human race, but it doesn't. Any pastor will vouch for the fact that leading most people to worship their Creator is something like asking for driving directions in Vermont. No matter how clearly you phrase the question, the reply will have something to do with heading "this-a-way," "just a bit," or "a far piece." In the end, you scratch your head and agree with the old saw: "You can't get there from here." Human beings are *incurvatus in se*, as Augustine and Luther put it, curved in upon themselves. For this reason, pastors can never assume that merely structuring worship according to a proper, biblical framework and then calling people to enter it will ensure that anyone will truly worship.

Worship never happens by accident, however. We arrive at authentic worship, as we arrive anywhere, by intending to go there and taking the steps that will move us forward. The confusing landscape of today's worship makes it all the more essential that we have some direction. That is why the task of theology is central to the pastoral vocation. Pastors who pay attention to the worship life of the church are "doing theology" in its most basic sense. I cringe at the often-heard dictum that "what the church needs is not more theology but more worship." The ancient church understood that *lex orandi, lex credendi*, the rule of prayer is the rule of faith. Theology is primarily a reflection upon worship; they are inseparable. To find our way in the current landscape of worship, we need more theology, not less.

Pastors who are determined to serve their roles as resident theologians must give primary attention to the phenomenon of culture and the way it affects the worship of the church. Anyone who doubts the relationship between culture and worship need look no further than Christmas, Easter, Halloween, or even, Mardi Gras to see the connection. All these festivals are rooted in the church's understanding of time and God's redemptive intentions for His world. Yet the church constantly finds itself fighting to preserve the true meaning of these sacred days. Halloween and Mardi Gras were ceded to the pagan culture long ago. Have we lost Christmas also? Lamin Sanneh, the Yale Divinity School missiologist, notes that part of Paul's legacy to the church was "exacting vigilance over the true nature of culture." Sanneh continues:

> Christian life is indelibly marked with the stamp of culture, and faithful stewardship includes uttering the prophetic word in culture, and sometimes even against it. Paul was a cultural iconoclast in his defiance of the absolutist tendencies in culture, but he was not a cultural cynic, for in his view God's purposes are mediated through particular cultural streams.[1]

This is sound direction for any pastor trying to safely navigate his or her church through the waters of contemporary culture. On the one hand, we cannot escape culture any more than a fish can stay dry in the ocean. We must be aware of the culture and how it shapes people, especially those attending our worship services. On the other hand, there is no reason to despair over the culture's godless tendencies. The world has always been turned away from God, and the gospel has always faced cultural challenges to its relevance. And the church has survived, even flourished, in times when the culture seemed most averse to it. We are not engaged in a human enterprise, after all. We rest in God's sovereignty. Yet, for reasons that have long both fascinated and mystified theologians, God has chosen to work through human agency. Thus, our vigilance in guarding and guiding worship is imperative.

With this in mind, we set out on our journey through Vermont. What is the current landscape against which worship is set? What are the cultural forces that affect our ability to lead people in authentic worship of the Creator? We will examine five: relativism, ritualism, rationalism, romanticism, and realism.

## RELATIVISM: WORSHIP DIVORCED FROM TRUTH

One of the most obvious characteristics of modern culture is its tendency toward *relativism*, the view that authoritative claims have validity only insofar as an individual chooses to grant such claims. This is one major symptom of the autonomous nature of modern and postmodern culture in which the individual is supreme and truth is defined as "whatever works for me."

This way of thinking has profound implications for those leading worship in the Christian tradition. Christianity, like all religions, makes truth claims about both itself and the world. Jesus claimed not only to *know* the truth but to *be* the truth. In John's gospel, Jesus tells the Samaritan woman that God seeks worshipers who will worship Him in spirit and in truth. These statements highlight the fundamental conflict between Christian worship and the regnant culture. As

Christian writers have acknowledged through the centuries and as the book of Acts demonstrates so readily, the Christian faith has a subversive relationship to culture. As the idol craftsmen in Ephesus discovered (see Acts 19), when people turn to Jesus it's bad for business. When that happens, the culture reacts. Any congregation that has the temerity to suggest that Jesus is Lord will find itself confronted by a culture that makes truth claims of its own.

What happens in that moment is, in many ways, the story of the church and of every individual pastor's ministry. Every pastor must answer the question "How will I relate to the culture around me?" The answer takes a practical cast nearly every week as pastors ask themselves, "What am I willing to do in order to attract people to church and hold their attention?" Cultural influence on pastoral integrity is most readily revealed in worship. There have been some well-intentioned efforts to answer these prickly questions that have essentially softened the Christian message so that it would not offend the culture. Even some reputable theologians and Bible scholars have attempted to make Scripture and the Christian faith more palatable to the modern person. These attempts have produced worship services that emphasize human self-actualization more than God's power to forgive human sin, often held in buildings devoid of any Christian symbols.

Against this landscape of softened truth claims, Paul's example is all the more vivid. The apostle never disregarded culture; in fact, he became "all things to all men in order to save some." Yet he knew that truth was a line not to be crossed in interacting with culture. Paul never failed to present the whole gospel, even on occasions when that message was deeply offensive to his hearers. To follow this example calls for great wisdom and sensitivity on the part of pastors. It requires highly developed analytical skill in exegeting the cultural scene and for genuine love and compassion for those caught up in the world outside the church.

One caution: pastors should avoid picking fights with the culture. The gospel will draw quite enough conflict on its own; we need not look for more. It is heartbreaking to see the misguided attempts of some churches to win a culture war that has little or no chance of displaying the power and grace of the Christian gospel. Flailing at windmills is not a good use of the church's energy. If those Christians who are leading the charge into postmodern culture are telling us anything, it is that we cannot despise the culture we are seeking to reach. Let us consider the example of Jesus, who was embraced by some elements from all sectors of the culture—both in the first century and today, in spite of the fact that He never compromised the truth He embodied.

The path of relativism is a tempting shortcut to reaching the culture, but in the end it leads nowhere. Speaking truth to the culture is precisely what the church is called to do. In doing so, we must be wise as serpents and gentle as doves. To speak the truth in love is the first imperative for leading modern people in the worship of God.

## RITUALISM: DIVORCING WORSHIP FROM LIFE

A second pressure the culture exerts on worship is *ritualism,* or the divorcing of worship from life. This is seen in the tendency of people to compartmentalize their lives in ways that serve their own interests. For example, pollsters routinely report that people who attend church regularly exhibit approximately the same moral behavior as those who do not. This suggests that people may relegate their faith to a certain compartment of their existence—their religious life. This neatly segmented approach to life produces a ritualistic approach to worship. Worship is an event that occupies an hour of time each week. It is a "nod to God," not to be confused with "real life," which takes place outside of church.

Ritualism was a rampant problem in ancient Israel and was noted particularly by the prophets. In his introduction to the Prophets in *The Message*, Eugene Peterson summarizes the phenomenon in words eerily applicable to our own day:

Everyone more or less believes in God. But most of us do our best to keep God on the margins of our lives or, failing that, refashion God to suit our convenience . . . One of the bad habits that we pick up early in our lives is separating things and people into secular and sacred. We assume that the secular is what we are more or less in charge of: our jobs, our time, our entertainment, our government, our social relations. The sacred is what God has charge of: worship and the Bible, heaven and hell, church and prayers. We then contrive to set aside a sacred place for God, designed, we say, to honor God but really intended to keep God in His place, leaving us free to have the final say about everything else that goes on.[2]

Ancient Israel's worship was characterized by preoccupation with religious activities accompanied by little concern for the ethical demands of the Covenant. A lot of people were "going to worship" but living life as they saw fit. It's a hereditary disposition issue to the children of Adam and Eve: We want to deal with God on our own terms. It is both ironic and frightening to consider that on any given weekend, a greater percentage of North Americans will be in church than any people in the world, yet on that same weekend more of our citizens will be murdered, more children abused, and more women violated than in any other "civilized" country. That is a symptom of ritualism. We go through motions of religious observance without truly submitting ourselves to God in worship.

The word *ritualism* has sometimes been used to decry the use of any rite within worship. That was not, however, the ritualism condemned by the prophets. A rite is simply a repeated series of acts, and all worship traditions have them. The problem is not with the rite but with practitioners who allow the rite to become meaningless. Isaiah 1 and Jeremiah 7, for example, clearly demonstrate that God was incensed about the lack of true righteousness in people who were performing religious customs with regularity and care. It was not the rites themselves that were the problem. Pastors know that simply reading the words of the marriage ceremony and asking the partners to make those timeless promises to one another does not guarantee that the marriage will last. Yet no one suggests that the marriage ceremony should be abolished. What we need to combat ritualism is not fewer rites but more meaning in our worship.

Ritualism has become a problem in modern worship precisely because of our tendency to separate life into what we believe are separate compartments, the sacred and the secular. The current culture has no quarrel with religion as long as it keeps to itself and doesn't try to impose its values on "real life." But, as the prophets point out, that way of living is neither biblically accurate nor ultimately practical. God is sovereign over all of life, and He expects to be involved in every aspect of human existence. To ignore that, sauntering into a church building for an hour or so a week believing that doing so fulfills our duty to God, is to turn our worship down the blind alley of ritualism. Pastors must be prophetic in calling their congregants to see that corporate worship on Sunday is not a retreat from normal life but is a continuation of worship and adoration, submission and obedience, that should characterize all of life. That is the kind of worship God seeks.

## RATIONALISM AND ROMANTICISM

Our technological society exerts two further pressures on worship, *rationalism*, and *romanticism*. The former results from overconfidence in human reason, and the latter is a reaction against that confidence. Theologian Donald Bloesch aptly summarizes the tension between what he calls rationalism and mysticism:

In rationalism we have an emphasis on the Word, but to the neglect of the spirit. In rationalistic milieu, the worship service is cerebral rather than affectional, didactic rather than kerygmatic. Sermons are reduced to lectures, thereby losing their character as announcements of good tidings . . . Sermons in this tradition frequently have a polemical or apologetic ring and are intended to persuade more than to convert . . .

In Mysticism, the worship service is designed to lead us into the presence of God, but without providing a rational grasp of who or what this presence is. The sermon often offers illumination in progressing in the Christian life, but not on clarifying the mysteries that constitute the foundation of faith. *Pneuma* and *praxis* take priority over *logos* in a radical or consistent mysticism.[3]

Bloesch correctly sees two distinct possibilities making their way into the church, one that guides action solely by the mind and the other guided by subjective interpretation. All worship planners will face pressure from these two forces.

## RATIONALISM: WORSHIP DIVORCED FROM MIND

God is honored when we use our minds; it is something we are created to do. Yet if reasonableness is used as the test for what we accept or reject in our spiritual lives, we have divorced worship from the realm of the spirit. Being overly bound by reason creates a malnourished spiritual life. I've worshiped in some overly rationalistic churches. Orthodox doctrine was emphasized, almost dogmatically, and the service was perfectly choreographed and aesthetically pleasing. Any worship element that did not appeal primarily to reason was considered suspect at best, shallow at worst. The ultimate taboo was any "loss of control" of the service by its leaders.

Yet Scripture asserts that our God is a consuming fire (Heb. 12:29) and that the Holy Spirit is like the wind, which blows wherever it wills (John 3:8). Jesus himself would not be bound by the grave for longer than three days. It is impossible for us to lose control of authentic worship, because we never had control to begin with. Pastors, who can be micromanagers, even control freaks (I speak as one), must be the first to acknowledge this. I am humbled to confess how often I've had to stifle my obsessive-compulsive desire to control what happens on Sunday morning and simply allow God to do what He intends to do. We must acknowledge that our rational faculties are offended by some of the things God wants us to do, such as loving our enemies and serving others. The grand paradox of the Christian faith is exemplified in the cross of Jesus Christ. Rationally speaking, it makes no sense to lay down one's life for others; yet Jesus did.

Worship that unduly elevates human wisdom will inevitably weaken the message of the Cross. Rationalistic worship is a feeble attempt to offer our ideas, our notions of spirituality, our conclusions about the world as a substitute for this God whose Spirit cannot be controlled in any way. And that's the real tension, isn't it? We enjoy worship as long as we are in control of it, but when God takes over, we become uncomfortable. Exodus 20:18–19 (RSV) describes the scene that took place immediately after Moses delivered the Ten Commandments to the people of Israel. It is a wonderfully revealing glimpse of human nature:

> Now when all the people perceived the thunderings and the lightnings and the sound of the trumpet and the mountain smoking, the people were afraid and trembled; and they stood afar off, and said to Moses, "You speak to us, and we will hear; but let not God speak to us, lest we die."

There is something about being in the presence of this uncontrollable God that makes an hour or so of the most boring preaching seem like a preferable option. As pastors, we want to lead our people into God's holy presence. That will not happen until we surrender all pretense of being able to dictate the terms of the encounter. We are not merely intellect wrapped in flesh and bones. We are spirit. There is a dimension of our being that goes beyond what can be touched or seen or heard, and we share that spiritual nature with the Creator.

This dimension of our beings must be addressed in worship. We must avoid the tantalizing desire to manage our journey into God's presence according to a roadmap of our own design.

### ROMANTICISM: WORSHIP DIVORCED FROM GOD

The reaction against rationalism can also be subversive of true worship. While Bloesch termed it *mysticism*, the term *romanticism* better describes the phenomenon I've observed in many modern churches. By romanticism, I mean the elevation of subjective experience—namely personal experience—is the controlling factor in the approach to worship. Worship guided by romanticism will eventually be divorced from its proper object, God, and fixed instead on some subjective state of mind or heart.

Postmodern people are numb from an overload of information. Their backlash against the cold, rationalistic, technological culture has been a retreat into the safety of personal experience. Romanticism says, in effect, "If I experienced it, it is real." This love of feeling and experience is the same as that seen in preteens who "fall in love with love." They are more enamored with the experience of being in love for the first time than with the actual person who is the ostensible object of their love.

This phenomenon is humorous and understandable in twelve-year-olds, but it is problematic as an approach to worship because our concept of God can so easily be captured by certain feelings or emotional states that He is effectively held hostage to our perceptions of Him. The danger is, as someone has put it, that we will stop worshiping God and start worshiping worship. Robb Redman writes, "Emotionally expressive worship has a strangely addictive quality for many. This may lead some to worship their worship experience rather than God. Moreover, many make their experience into a benchmark for others."[4]

I grew up in a church where expressive worship was the norm. Being an introverted and outwardly unemotional person, I often felt alienated from what happened on Sunday mornings, so much so that I was unsure whether I could embrace Christianity. Thankfully, I soon came to understand that worship can legitimately be expressed in a number of ways, emotion being only one of them. That early experience demonstrated the downside of evaluating worship by our emotional response to what happens in the service. As Thomas Long reminds us, "God does not always move us, and everything that moves us is not God."[5] Certainly there is feeling in worship. God made us as emotional creatures and He intends for that aspect of our being to be present and accounted for in worship. Yet it is a mistake to associate "real worship" with one particular experience that may or may not have been an authentic movement of God. What is worse, we may hold others to that same, subjective standard. That is not at all what the Bible says about "real" worship, which is a matter of both spirit and truth.

When people leave our churches each week evaluating the worship service on the basis of what they experienced or how they felt about it, they are acting upon romantic notions about God that are in fact an obstacle to worship. Even more problematic, that approach to worship easily becomes the worship of self. This is one of the major criticisms leveled at much of the "new style" worship. Some of that criticism, to be sure, is a manifestation of the more rationalistic, controlling, approach to worship. Still, the question must be asked: Who is the object of our worship—God or us?

Don Bloesch observes that much contemporary worship is marked by what he calls *eros spirituality*, the desire to possess the highest good. He writes, "This is especially evident in contemporary music in which love is portrayed in terms of passion and longing for God. The paradigm is the solitary individual in union with God . . . New style worship is concerned not with the people of God who unite their voices in a tribute of gratitude and adoration to God, but with the seeker after God who aspires to rise above the pressures and trials of living in the world in order to be lost in 'wonder love and praise.'"[6]

Bloesch overgeneralizes where contemporary music is concerned, but he does have a point. Too often corporate worship is lost in the attempt of individuals to plug into God at their own level. While the move toward more experiential worship is clearly a trend in the church that must be taken seriously, pastors would be foolish to ignore the danger of allowing yet one more manifestation of the self curved back on itself. As one old preacher put, "Satan doesn't mind us worshiping, he just doesn't want us worshiping God."

The first commandment is abundantly clear on this point: "You shall have no other gods before me" (Exod. 20:3). And when He was tempted, Jesus told Satan, "You shall worship the Lord your God and him only shall you serve" (Matt. 4:10 RSV). Theodore Jennings said that "if we settle for less than God, we're likely to make that less into God and thus, God becomes the guarantor of the way things are. This is the idolatry of those who have settled down in the land—who transform Yahweh into Baal."[7] The reference to Baal at this point is not coincidental in the least. A number of biblical and liturgical scholars draw analogues between Israel's emphasis on intensive experience in worship and its struggle with Baalism. That was the predominant form of worship in Canaan when Israel entered the land, and Baal worship emphasized subjective experience. The idol being worshiped was secondary to the experience of the worshiper; the objective reality, the god, was subordinated to the religious passions of the devotee. Thomas Long notes that in the Old Testament, the hiddenness of God is one of the key distinctions between Yahwism and Baalism.[8] Baal was always present and always available to provide ecstatic experience. Perhaps predictably, cult prostitution flourished in the worship of Baal. For those to whom sensory experience was the crucial element of worship, sexual activity became the highest form of religious expression.

This is more than an interesting bit of biblical history; it is a reminder that it is extremely dangerous to enthrone the self as the object of worship so that intense personal experience becomes the magnetic attraction to worship, rather than the reality of God. The lesson to pastors and worship leaders is clear: Focus on God, not the feelings of the people. The presence of God will generate all the feeling and experience anyone could desire. Perhaps Jesus' teaching that we find ourselves only when we lose ourselves applies also to worship. Romanticism, like the rationalism that it displaces, is a false direction for worship.

## REALISM: WORSHIP DIVORCED FROM ITSELF

A final cultural force affecting the direction of worship is *realism*, which divorces worship from itself. By realism, I refer to the peculiarly contemporary phenomenon of attempting to convince worshipers that it is practical or useful for them to attend church on Sunday morning. Realism is the attempt to find utility in worship, to make it useful as a means to some other end. Realism has given us worship experiences crafted around such themes as "Six Steps to Financial Freedom" and "How to Drug-Proof Your Kids." While those may be good and useful pursuits, they don't depend in any way upon God. And that's the point. Worship is about God, period. It is what Marva Dawn so wonderfully called "a royal waste of time." It has no purpose, no utility, no value other than as our response to God for His gracious acts of salvation. Attempts to use worship for some other end are at best futile and at worst dangerous. Worship has value for its own sake, and nothing else.

In our what's-the-cash-value culture, the idiosyncratic value of worship can be a significant problem. Brian McClaren asks if this problem of keeping people interested in worship might be the natural result of employing evangelistic programs that are designed to appeal to the self-interests of people. Can such an introduction to the faith fail to produce self-centered, consumeristic worshipers?[9] The consumer impulse runs deep in our culture, and pastors must continually guard against the temptation to accommodate worship to the felt needs of people, continually trying to convince them that "we're only here to get something of value to take back into the real world."

In fact, sitting in a sanctuary with others of like faith is about as *real* as it gets. There is no need to apologize for asking people to devote time to nothing else but offering praise and worship to the Creator of the universe. Attending church is not necessarily a more spiritual activity than other things we do as human beings, but there are few activities that are so intentionally directed away from ourselves as is worship. That is our justification for worship, if one is needed. As Karl Barth might well have said, the only excuse we need for worship is that God is God. Worship is its own reward. Even so, I have discovered that when I give myself wholeheartedly to this "scandalously useless activity," there is a result—I am transformed. Again, when we lose our lives, we find them.

## GETTING THERE FROM HERE

The cultural forces that affect worship are like computer viruses, embedded in the hard drive of a computer and waiting to be activated. These forces—relativism, ritualism, rationalism, romanticism, and realism—are ever-present because we are broken, sinful people, and each of them appeals to some aspect of our fallen nature. The ultimate expression of sin is idolatry, and idolatry reveals itself as the enthronement of self. It is intriguing that the apostle John ends his first epistle with the words "Little children, keep yourselves from idols." John was a wise and discerning pastor, for as Luther observed, "Idols are, in the last resort, a form of human self-worship: I give value to what I choose. The God-given capacity to love turns in upon itself and becomes human self-love: *homo incurvatus in se*."[10]

Pastors should not wonder then, that leading worship is not easy. What worthwhile endeavor is? I've conducted enough worship services to realize that no matter how carefully we plan the experience, many will miss the point because they are too busy looking at themselves in the mirror. For this reason, we need authentic worship all the more, worship that will shift our focus away from ourselves and toward God, worship that will transport us—both mind and spirit—into His transforming presence, worship that will change us.

Yes, some Sundays, leading worship is like driving in Vermont— you're never quite sure if it is possible to get there from here. Indeed, is it possible to usher our people into the presence of the One who can enable them to transcend the narrowness of the culture and gain a God's-eye perspective of themselves and their world? The very possibility makes me eager to draw up yet another set of directions.

## CHAPTER FOUR

# LEADERSHIP

## *It Doesn't Matter if You Can't Sing*

—ɯ—

*For good or ill, the worship leader's presence and style sets the tone for worship.*
—Thomas Long

### SILVER BULLET
Congregations benefit from strong pastoral leadership in worship.

S unday worship at the church I attended as a child had three distinct parts. The centerpiece was preaching, of course. That was followed by an altar call, what liturgists would describe as the response to the Word. Everything else was labeled "preliminaries." That included all congregational singing, prayer, announcements, and offerings. These things seemed unimportant in their own right and served only to set the stage for the sermon. I recall walking in to the church twenty minutes or so before the service one Sunday and watching the song leader and pianist, heads together, choose music for the service. I now cringe when I think of the imbalanced worship that approach could, and sometimes did, produce. Beyond the liturgical inadequacy of that method, it produced in me a highly unrealistic view of the pastor's world. I can't remember my pastor ever being involved in the preliminaries, except to offer a prayer or a brief exhortation about the offering. From what I could tell, all my pastor needed to be concerned about were the sermon and altar call. My, how the times have changed!

Given the changes afoot in twenty-first century worship and the fact that worship is often the port of entry into the church, the role of the pastor in conducting worship has changed dramatically. No longer can a pastor afford to focus solely on his or her sermon and the response to it. Pastors have to be involved in planning the entire worship service, which is rightly expected to form a coherent whole. The old pastoral excuse for abdicating leadership of worship music—"I can't sing"—has no standing these days. Pastors must be involved in strategic ways with every aspect of worship. Any pastor who surrenders to others ultimate responsibility for leading the worship of the church will get exactly what he or she deserves.

Technically speaking, the subjects I teach are called practical theology. That is not, as some have impishly suggested, an oxymoron. I, as all pastors must be, am a pastoral theologian. Pastoral theology is the application of theological convictions to inform and define the work of the pastor. It is theology in its purest form, theology applied to life. Pastors are the resident theologians of their congregations, the theological gatekeepers, charged with insuring that the congregation pays sufficient attention to and is formed by the meta-narratives of historic Christianity rather than the latest fads of the twenty-first-century culture.

John Calvin ordered the pastoral role according to the Old Testament offices of prophet, priest, and king. The prophetic office arose with Moses and developed heightened visibility in the days of the kings. This office is most readily connected with proclamation and teaching, and most pastors devote significant time and energy to these ministerial tasks. The kingly office, in Calvin's thinking, referred to administrative and leadership issues that affect the well-being of the people. The story of the kings in ancient Israel was the story of the entire nation. If the king followed the Covenant and "walked in the ways of the Lord," Israel experienced the blessing of God. If the king disobeyed and led the people astray, the entire nation suffered. Prophets most often aimed their messages at the kings, pointing out their responsibility for the sad state of God's people. The current interest in leadership within the church is well founded. Leadership clearly makes a difference.

The priestly office is probably the least understood in the Protestant tradition because it is so readily associated with Roman Catholicism. But the priestly ministry is well attested from the time of Aaron on, and the priestly functions are critical to the pastoral vocation. A priest is one who mediates, or stands between, God and human beings. Aaron and his sons served on behalf of the people, performing worship acts that required special preparation, symbolic presence, or ritual holiness. Of course, Jesus Christ has become our ultimate High Priest and mediates our relationship with God in a way that no earthly priest could. Nevertheless, the priestly elements within pastoral ministry remain vital, and overseeing the church's worship is a crucial element of that priestly role. To serve the people by providing worship that genuinely turns people to God is the most visible aspect of priestly ministry for a pastor.

Marva Dawn convincingly argues that since worship is the only thing the church does that no one else can do, worship should be a congregation's top priority.[1] That will never be the case unless pastors accept their role as priests and give due attention to worship leadership. Regardless of who leads the songs or reads the Scriptures, it is the pastor who sets the tone for the liturgy. The pastor is the worship leader of the church.

## BENEFITS OF PASTORAL LEADERSHIP

Courses on worship are routinely required in ministerial education programs and in preparation for ordination. This emphasis upon the priestly office marks a dramatic shift in ministerial education. Thirty or so years ago, ministerial preparation included very little instruction on worship leadership. Evangelism and preaching were the prime concerns. We are now reaping the harvest of that inadequate sowing as consumer-driven evangelism and effective communication (versus prophetic preaching) now dominate the worship of the church. Today, no one would dream of construing ministerial education without including an emphasis on worship. It is too important to neglect. Sometimes the old ways aren't the best ways. Pastoral leadership of the church's worship is vitally important.

## IT PROTECTS WORSHIP FROM IMPROPER LEADERSHIP

Proverbs 29:18 (NASB) reads, "Where there is no vision, the people are unrestrained." Those words call to mind a number of disturbing images for those of us in ministry. The kind of unbridled desire and lack of restraint that characterizes modern culture has proven destructive to the people under our ministerial charges. Consider the consequences of that same lack of restraint in the church's worship. Imagine the likely result when a pastor abdicates leadership of worship, turning it over to, say, a new believer whose primary qualification is that he once played lead guitar in a rock band. If that scenario is an exaggeration, it is only a slight one. Which of us hasn't endured a "worship service," all the while wondering what the pastor could have been thinking to have put such an inexperienced and unqualified person in charge of so crucial a part of the congregation's life? Admittedly, pastors have much to do and priorities must be set. Involving others in ministry is both scriptural and necessary. Yet to busy oneself with other things while the worship life of the church dies a slow and painful death is inexcusable, especially given the kinds of resources available to pastors today.

Pastoral leadership of worship is an important protection against the hijacking of worship by an individual or clique within the church. John Lukacs has described the church today as moving from the tyranny of the majority to the rule of the minority in the name of the majority. "What counts," he says, "is what people want/people don't know what they want/experts know what people want/people are told what they want/people want what they are told."² Lukacs has just described the function of many church worship committees. Pastoral leadership is needed to ensure that the worship life of the church reflects the congregation's legitimate needs and preferences and not merely the desires of those who have managed to gain control of the liturgy.

## It Provides Pastoral Care

Pastors who give proper attention to the worship of the congregation discover the best way of helping their people cope with life. To turn aside from the demands of the week and devote oneself to God is among the most important means for living wholly and vitally amid modern culture. Cultural critic Os Guinness has observed that in our frantic modern life,

> Time is the ultimate credit card, speed is the universal style of spending and "the faster the better" is the ideal tempo of life. Call it "craziness" call it the "curse of our age" call it the "tyranny of the urgent" call it anything you like. But it is impossible to stop the world today even if you want to get off and its manic speed is affecting our faith as much as our blood pressure.³

The call to worship God is a call to step out of the frantic rat race we call modern life. To enable our people to truly experience the restful Sabbath of God's presence is a crucial element of pastoral care and an unmistakable sign of our love for them.

After eighteen years of pastoral service and more than ten years of preparing men and women for the pastorate, I find myself in lockstep agreement with William Willimon, who contends that worship is a major, if neglected, aspect of pastoral care.⁴ As I reflect on my pastoral tenure, I believe that the attention I gave to public worship allowed me to flourish in pastoral service despite my significant weaknesses in areas usually considered fundamental for ministry. Leading people effectively in worship will buy for the pastor a lot of grace in other areas of ministry. The effort expended by the pastor in public worship is never misspent.

## IT ENHANCES PREACHING

As one who both teaches preaching and found the pulpit to be his pastoral niche, I am interested to observe the fact that the sermon can no longer compel attendance at worship and cannot "save the liturgy" in the way it did as few as twenty years ago. This is not to downgrade the significance of preaching or the attention pastors should give to it. I simply recognize that the ecclesial landscape is changing in many ways, and the role of the sermon is one of them. Willimon alludes to this changing environment:

Protestant seminaries, dominated for decades by pulpit centered worship, . . . neglected to prepare ministers for competent worship leadership. We were misled into thinking that the artful proclamation of the Word in the Sunday sermon was enough to feed a congregation for a lifetime. The burden of having to make worship happen "ex nihilo" for one's congregation Sunday after Sunday wears heavily upon the Free Church minister.[5]

Most pastors will recognize the reality behind Willimon's phrase "make worship happen 'ex nihilo.'" To take upon oneself the entire burden of producing every week a sermon good enough to inspire, sustain, and give legitimacy to the entire worship endeavor is an impossible task. To attempt it is to risk disaster, or burnout, or both. Whenever I think of creating worship ex nihilo, I recall the day in graduate school when I realized that something was amiss in my pastoral preparation. I was a theology student in a Roman Catholic institution, and one day I overheard a group of nuns discussing a new priest who had arrived. "So what do you think of Father So-and-so?" one asked. "He's all right, I guess," was the reply. "He says a good mass."

As a twenty-six-year-old pastor who was trying to figure out how to jump-start next Sunday's worship, I was filled with envy and wonder at the idea that some worship leaders had no need to recreate the liturgy each week. Happily, many younger ministers in our tradition are figuring this out sooner than I did and are recovering the value of liturgy.

Preaching is not to be devalued, however. In spite of how preaching is changing, in many ways for the better, there is no reason to think that the proclamation of the Word of God will lose its significant place in the worship of the church. Sermon preparation takes every bit as much time as it ever did, if not more, in these new liturgical surroundings. The current state of preaching in many churches is sadly disappointing. It is an easy resort to blame colleges and seminaries for this homiletical debacle. In the workaday world of the pastor, the time required to create good preaching is often sacrificed to a myriad of other pastoral duties. If we are to both improve the church's worship and place a right priority on the craft of preaching, then pastors will need to reexamine how they spend their time. Given the fact that the Sunday worship service is the pastor's prime time with most congregation members, pastors cannot afford to devalue worship planning and preaching preparation. The casual way in which many of us approach both tasks must truly perplex laypeople. The public leadership of worship is the one pastoral activity that every pastor is expected to be able to do and is an activity that laypeople always list near the top of all pastoral activities.[6]

## PRINCIPLES FOR WORSHIP LEADING

When taking leadership of worship, pastors must be committed to allowing the Holy Spirit to set the agenda for worship, rather than inserting their own. In most attempts to "fix" worship, we are likely to grab too readily for anything that promises to solve the problem. Often, that takes the form of a fundraising drive or other agenda that is imposed upon worship. Worship becomes a kind of liturgical trial and error as we search for the perfect solution for holding people's attention on Sunday mornings. C. S. Lewis reminds all of us innovators that "the charge is 'feed my sheep,' not 'run experiments on my rats.'"[7] The danger in experimentation is not only the harm it does to congregational worship but also the harm it does to the pastor's credibility with thoughtful persons in the church. They soon begin to see that they are being used to fulfill some agenda other than the praise and adoration of God. No capital campaign or membership drive is worth paying that kind of price.

The reason we are tempted to tinker with worship, of course, is that in too many cases it is anemic or even boring. The danger is that in seeking to revive worship, we as pastors will become absolutely pragmatic, selling ourselves for anything that seems to work. Yet God is not boring! When it seems so, the problem is more likely to do with people's inability to truly connect with God than with liturgical traditions or musical styles. I took on a small country church a few years ago as part-time pastor. There were twenty-six worship attendees on my first Sunday there. At the end of my four-year tenure, there were often some two hundred worshipers crammed into a building that would comfortably house about eighty. We sang very little contemporary music and had almost no performance music or any liturgical innovations. When surveyed, the answer most often given by worshipers for attending there was that God was clearly present in the services. The most effective thing pastors can do as worship leaders is not to implement new methods or create innovative liturgy but to help people become connected to God.

In his invaluable little book *Beyond the Worship Wars,* Thomas Long cites a study that identified the characteristics of vital and faithful congregations. In particular, the worship life of these churches was observed. The churches represented a number of denominations, and their worship styles ranged from formal to Pentecostal. The study yielded nine characteristics of worship that were shared by these vital congregations.[8] These characteristics are useful for examining the ways pastors can exercise leadership in worship in a manner that will both strengthen their churches and honor God. Here are ways that pastors can help their people be connected to God without resorting to fads or gimmickry, and without imposing their own agendas upon worship.

## MAKE ROOM FOR MYSTERY

While the subject of postmodern culture can be a minefield of debatable and unwarranted assumptions, it is indisputable that our current culture longs for the transcendent. People want to experience a God who is bigger than they are. And this necessarily involves the element of mystery. Yet from the all-too-common opening words—"Good morning. Ahem, I said *Good morning!*"—to the benediction, delivered with the enthusiasm usually reserved for a financial report, there is no mystery, no transcendence, and nothing that awes or thrills in the typical evangelical worship service. Marva Dawn issues this stern critique:

> It is surely important for the clergy to be friendly with the parish rather than austere and distant as many pastors once were—but the pendulum has now swung so far in the opposite direction that many congregations seem to have become the private cults of the charismatic leader. I'm stating the extreme here, but it is because I fear the subtle replacement of the mystery of the Trinity, with the pastor's personality in initiating worship. It is almost as if the priest invites us into his living room instead of God welcoming us into His presence. I suggest that a pastoral greeting and the necessary announcements be made first to establish the community and that the turn into actual worship be decisively made by urging the congregation to let the prelude lead them into God's presence, or by a statement like, "now we give all our attention to God, Who has called us here in the name of . . ."[9]

To recapture the sense of mystery is to take the role of worship leader seriously, realizing that you have the ability to shape the attitude of the worshipers in any given service. People don't want firm answers so much as they want to know there is a God out there who can help them deal with their questions. They want God more than they want steps to financial freedom or foolproof principles for parenting, at least they'd want that if they were being taken into God's awesome presence with any regularity. Recapture the mystery as a leader.

## SHOW HOSPITALITY

Showing hospitality to strangers sets the stage for worship, and this involves more than posting greeters in the foyer each week. The New Testament understanding of hospitality is to identify the "strangers" in our midst and make them welcome. This is the legitimate point behind what has been called seeker sensitivity. Yet seeker-sensitive worship easily becomes seeker driven. Re-creating the liturgy for the benefit of those outside the church is neither authentic hospitality nor good worship. Healthy churches find ways to make others feel welcome without allowing the worship service to degenerate into a lounge act. In fact, the seeker approach can be counterproductive in some ways, as Terri Bocklund McLean observes.

> A major criticism of alternative or contemporary worship is that it is a spectator event, driven by entertainment minded, presentation style leadership. This trap must be avoided by worship planners and leaders. Presentation style worship requires nothing of the people and those gathered for worship need not give anything of themselves back to God.[10]

To be hospitable to strangers in worship does not entail offering to them something less than the amazing gospel. Finding new ways to do that, however, is always worthy of investigation.

## RECOVER A SENSE OF DRAMA

The gospel is a dramatic story, and worship leaders can enhance worship by making that drama visible. This includes both the content of worship and the use of the Christian calendar—issues that will be examined in depth later in this book. To lead worship effectively, pastors must be aware of how they can help or hinder in creating a sense of drama for worshipers. I read about a pastor who embodied this sense of drama during the Christmas Eve service. His demeanor, tone, and body language as he opened the service were that of someone who was about to share the best news ever. The tone was infectious.

Christmas, Easter, Pentecost—these are dramatic occasions. I've often been tempted to enter the chancel on a Sunday morning with a large rope tied around my leg, just as the priests of Israel did when entering the Holy of Holies. The rope would serve to remind the people that I was about to serve God on their behalf, and that can be dangerous. The rope could be used to drag me out in case things didn't go well. Annie Dillard's well-known quip about ushers passing out crash helmets and issuing life preservers to worshipers who are about to enter the presence of God captures the sense of drama associated with any gathering where Yahweh is present. One role of the pastor in leading worship is to help communicate that.

## USE EXCELLENT, ECLECTIC MUSIC

Many pastors do not know much about music—a failing that musicians love to point out to us! The subject is important enough to occupy two later chapters of this book; but for now, a word about pastoral leadership in this area. It doesn't matter if you can't sing! Pastors are the worship leaders in their churches and must give attention to this aspect of worship regardless of the level of their own musical ability. Strong music ministries do not typically develop apart from strong pastoral leadership. Pastors are in the best position to know both the theological significance of music in the church and the musical tastes and capabilities of their congregations. At a minimum, pastors can work with the leaders of the church to produce, in writing if necessary a coherent statement on what this church is trying to accomplish musically in its worship. All church musicians must be held accountable to that policy—with no exceptions. No pastor was ever more "musically challenged" than I. Yet I attest that it is possible to oversee the music of the church in such a way that the mission of the church is served—even if you don't know a half-note from a quarter-rest.

Oversight of music includes emphasizing both excellence in what music is done and variation in what selections are offered. Eclectic selection does not imply randomness. There are some churches where Bach might never be appropriate, and some in which bluegrass would never be effective. That is why the pastor is in a position to make a reasonable decision about such matters. Great care needs to be exercised in this area, and a dictatorial approach is not likely to do well. But pastors are the legitimate authority in all matters of worship in the local church, including music, and they should exercise that authority.

## ADAPT WORSHIP SPACE

Few pastors have the luxury of designing their own worship facilities. Most inherit a worship space that was created for another day—or century. But with some creativity and with the blessing of their congregations, pastors can often adapt space in a way that fosters an atmosphere for worship. Helping people to respond in worship with their whole selves, including the senses of sight, touch, hearing, and even smell, helps them realize that worship is intended to encompass all dimensions of human life. The smell of baking bread, for example, could create a powerful environment for presenting Jesus as the Bread of Life. Providing some direction to the flower committee, or whoever takes responsibility for the visual aspects of the sanctuary, can create an appropriate look for a given worship service.

## CONNECT WORSHIP AND MISSION

Vital congregations find a way to forge a strong connection between worship and the local mission of the church. That connection is expressed in every aspect of the worship service. I often ask pastors to tell me about the community in which their churches are located. Their answers reveal a great deal about the pastors and their ministries. One of the unpardonable sins of pastoral ministry is to know nothing of the surrounding community. A second error, inevitable after committing the first, is the failure to include relevant aspects of that community in the worship experience. For example, a pastor serving in an ethnic community who does not include some ethnic customs or music in worship sends the message that he or she is completely disconnected from the community. Nearly all of pastoral theology is summed up in Jesus' words "I know my sheep and my sheep know me" (John 10:14). Knowing one's people and exegeting one's community is a key to constructing worship services that connect people with God. The saying "all politics are local" might well be applied to worship. Understanding the local setting is vital for leading worship, which is why a one-size-fits-all approach to worship planning will never be widely successful.

## CREATE STABILITY

Healthy and vital churches maintain a relatively stable order of service and have a significant repertoire of worship elements and responses that the congregation knows by heart. The nature of these things differs from church to church, and what might seem like comfortable, free-flowing worship in one church can appear to be chaotic or disordered by the standards of another congregation. Yet it is good for churches to develop their own rituals, traditions, and styles of spiritual life.

Oversight by the pastor is critical for creating this stability and continuity within a congregation's worship. For example, the pastor may find it necessary to remind adventurous musicians to stay within congregational parameters, lest the congregation get lost musically. One of the most important aspects of worship leadership is to be aware of how a particular group of people responds to God. This isn't to say that these practices are written in stone and form the liturgical destiny of that church. Yet these local traditions form the starting point for worship life and for meaningful change. To change those elements too soon is among the most common and costly mistakes made by inexperienced pastors.

## CREATE A JOYOUS CELEBRATION

Like any good story, the gospel has a climax. Good worship creates a joyous and climactic festival experience somewhere near the end of a service. The shape of that experience depends on the community itself—its local traditions, mission, and particular concerns. Christian worship is ultimately permeated with hope and joy. This doesn't preclude the honesty of confession or lament, but it does focus on the hopefulness of the gospel as its benediction. Pastors must have direct input in constructing this joyous, celebrative moment. As worship leaders, we want our people to grasp the true character of the God they have been worshiping. Even when dealing with pain and heartache, congregations should be willing to place these matters into the greater context of the good news of Jesus Christ.

## LEAD WITH STRENGTH AND ENERGY

Long's study found that healthy churches have strong, charismatic pastors as worship leaders. I winced a bit upon reading that. The phrase conjured for me the image of a televangelist, gaudily dressed, prancing Elmer Gantry–like before a spellbound congregation. While it is impossible to manipulate God, it is all too easy to manipulate people. All worship leaders, ordained or lay, need to understand how easy it is to fall into the role of fabricating an experience rather than guiding an authentic encounter with God. Having taken that concern seriously, however, we recognize that there is a necessary place for strong pastoral leadership in worship. Long clarifies:

> The fact that congregations build up membership by showcasing their pastors' winning personalities on Sunday morning, or by putting their ministers on television in an attempt to make them

celebrities is one of the worst features of church life in our society. However, the protest of theologians aside, the raw truth of the matter is that the personality and gifts of personal leadership do matter, they matter to the quality of congregational life, to the attractiveness of the church, to visitors, and to the total ethos of worship.[11]

They are people of deep integrity who have the power to bless others, the willingness to act in Christlike ways as they lead, and the ability to allow a service of worship to be a place of honest hospitality and the sharing of gifts.[12]

The effective leadership of worship by a pastor depends ultimately on his or her character, integrity, and spiritual depth. The ability to lead public worship is secured only by private worship in the study. Those who are intimately connected with God will capably lead others in finding a connection with Him.

Helpfully, Long mentions four principles worship leaders should embody.[13] First, the worship leader should establish positive, personal connection with the congregation. This is more than smarmy friendliness. This is at the heart of the priestly office. The ability to instill confidence in the congregants that here is a leader who can skillfully mediate the presence of God, however needed. Second, the leader should gather the gifts of the congregation. This makes knowing the church crucial. Most churches have more resources than they are aware of. Good pastoral leaders identify these resources so they can benefit the church. Third, the primary leader should share the leadership of worship with others. Perhaps the single most important change to affect worship in the twenty-first century will be the emphasis on participation. People are no longer content to be passive spectators — they want to participate. Finally, the worship leader should exemplify holiness. A carefully crafted worship experience may be lost in a moment of careless irreverence or thoughtless buffoonery. There's a time to be casual before a congregation; there are also times when decorum and professionalism are required. Knowing the difference between those moments is essential.

Being a competent leader in worship involves a combination of liturgical protocol and good old common sense. At its best, it also combines aspects of both the priestly and prophetic office. The pastor as priest leads the people in experiencing the mystery of God's holiness. The pastor as prophet warns of the need for holy living in—but not of— the world. Both offices are needed, as Daniel Frankforter notes: "The priest commands the faithful to kneel in prayer before altars while the prophet orders them into the streets to fight injustice."[14] Balanced pastoral leadership in worship is an invaluable step in church health and in enabling modern congregations to navigate both the treacherous shoals of culture and the potential minefields of the worship wars. Prophet, priest, and king—there's nothing in that job description about being able to sing. It is about the willingness to lead.

## CHAPTER FIVE

# LITURGY

## *Defining the Work of the People*

—ɯ—

*One of the underlying issues in worship renewal is the
need to return worship to the people. A passive approach
to worship has slowly seeped into the church over the
past several centuries, and many contemporary Christians
have grown up believing that worship is something done
for them rather than something they do themselves.*
—Robert Webber

### SILVER BULLET
Good liturgy transforms spectators into participants.

A s a kid, my favorite job at our church was to hand out the
Sunday bulletins. I confess that I volunteered for this task
mostly because it gave me the chance to linger outside in the narthex
long after the service began, "just in case" someone came in late.
Looking back, I suspect that this auspicious chore could be entrusted
to someone of my mixed motivations only because there was nothing
of real importance in the bulletin—at least nothing that had anything to
do with the worship taking place in the sanctuary. Our church bulletins
were always printed on store-bought stock and featured a colorful

photo of a beautiful church building or a serene nature scene superimposed with a Bible verse. Inside was the usual information about service times, announcements about Sunday school picnics, and, thanks to a vintage mimeograph machine, a collection of ink blots that might have inspired the Rorschach test. There was nothing in our Sunday bulletins that gave the least hint of what would happen in that Sunday's worship. That, we claimed with a certain amount of pride, was up to the Holy Spirit.

The very idea of publishing an order of worship was viewed as the first step on the slippery slope to Unitarianism. Orders of service were for churches that we labeled with the dreaded L-word—liturgical. Or liberal. In our view, the terms were synonymous. Liturgy, we had been taught, was empty ritual, a "smells and bells" approach to worship that signaled a rejection of the Holy Spirit's leadership. Liturgical churches, so the rumor went, printed their orders of service because they had given up on the idea of experiencing God and were just going through the motions. Churches like ours, so we thought, where the only practical use for a bulletin was to start a fire, were the only *real* churches around.

The claim was ignorant, of course, and incredibly arrogant. It was also absurd given the fact that there was a very precise order to our services each Sunday. Any attendee who took note could easily have observed that our services followed a definite pattern and could have predicted the next item in our unwritten order of service with 90 percent accuracy. Even the most "spontaneous" of congregations have some understanding of how they will conduct public worship. That order may not be written for everyone to see, but those who lead worship know it and know it well.

Fear of the L-word, or, more accurately, a total misunderstanding of it, locked my boyhood church into an approach to worship that was not only incomplete but also more confining than that of the most formally ritualized churches over whom we pretended spiritual superiority.

Liturgy is not a dirty word.

All churches are liturgical churches in that they necessarily employ some basic model or rubric by which to structure worship. In his book *The Worship Maze*, Paul Basden categorizes modern worship styles by the terms *liturgical, traditional, revivalist,* and *seeker.*[1] Many congregations think of themselves as fitting neatly into one of these categories, yet it may be misleading to apply the term *liturgical* so narrowly. All worship is liturgical, out of necessity, since all worship is expressed using various forms, images, and actions. The distinction between "liturgical" and "nonliturgical" worship is a false one.

The question surrounding liturgy, then, is not whether churches will employ it. All churches do. The real liturgical question for worship leaders is whether the liturgy employed will be *good* liturgy or *bad* liturgy. Good liturgy is that which achieves the aim of enabling people to engage in biblical worship. Bad liturgy—however excellently executed, culturally relevant, or just plain hip it might be—is that which falls short of the goal of bringing a congregation meaningfully into God's presence. Recovering a true sense of liturgy—good liturgy—is the key to revitalizing worship.

## 'GOOD' VERSUS 'BAD' LITURGY

The word *liturgy* is not properly a worship or even a theological term. The term is derived from the Greek word *leitorgeia*, which was composed from two Greek roots, one meaning *work* and the other *people*. Liturgical scholar James White offers this definition:

> In ancient Greece, a liturgy was a public work, something performed for the benefit of the city or state. Its principle was the same as that of paying taxes, but it could involve donated services as well as taxes. Paul speaks of the Roman authorities literally as "liturgists of God" (Rom. 13:6) and himself as a liturgist of Christ Jesus to the Gentiles (Rom. 15:16). Liturgy, then, is a work performed by the people for the ben-

efit of others. In other words, it is the quintessence of the priesthood of all believers in which the whole priestly community of Christians shares. To call a service liturgical is to indicate that it was conceived so that all worshipers take an active part and all may worship together.[2]

By defining liturgy as a work performed *by* the people *for* others, White clearly directs worship away from the passive, performance orientation that it has often taken in recent times and toward an active, participatory service rendered by the entire congregation.

## GOD AS THE AUDIENCE

Danish philosopher Søren Kierkegaard's analogy is useful at this point. Kierkegaard compares worship to a theater, but one that is different from what we are used to. Rather than picturing the congregation as the audience, passively absorbing the performance of the pastor, musicians, and other actors in the worship drama, Kierkegaard portrays God himself as the audience of worship, while the pastor and musicians function as prompters or coaches for the entire congregation, who are themselves the actors, directing every act and word toward God.[3]

When viewed this way, Christian worship takes on subtle yet significant nuances that are otherwise overlooked. For example, the sermon is "not just the gift of the preacher, nor are choral gifts simply the contributions of the choir, but both involve the offering of themselves by all the members of the congregation."[4] Carlton R. Young says that

We often tend to treat the choir as if it were the congregation whereas, we ought instead, to treat the congregation as if it were the choir. The choir is always only a supplement to the congregation except at sacred concerts. The choir exists only to do what the congregation cannot accomplish or to help the congregation do its singing better. Choral music is not a substitute for congregational song.[5]

In some ways the praise and worship movement has been a significant step in restoring liturgy in the original sense of the word, namely the work of the people.[6]

## PEOPLE AS 'ACTORS'

In most of the churches I've been associated with, music has sometimes been allowed to cross the line of liturgical propriety in ways that did not serve the best interests of the congregation. All music—including performance music that we sometimes refer to as "special" music—should be examined according to that standard. James White notes,

> When simply dropped in as a musical interlude to cover some action or worse still, as a bit of entertainment, it is highly questionable. When the anthem functions as a musical commentary on God's Word, it can be a strong asset to worship. Even then, it ought not deprive the congregation the opportunity of singing hymns and songs.[7]

In the small church I most recently led as pastor, we typically did not have special music precisely because I was concerned about establishing the congregation as the primary actors in worship. Recovering the fundamentally participatory nature of authentic worship is critical for revitalizing the worship of the local church. In interviews with worship attendees, Don Saliers identified a disturbing pattern. Interviewees consistently named three conditions that hindered their participation in worship. They were (1) when worship is "done for us," (2) when worship is "done to us," and (3) when "we don't understand" what is happening in worship.[8] All three conditions recall an image of a medieval cathedral in which laypeople sit passively, mystified by the curious motions of the priest, saying mass in Latin. The image is not so different from the modern worship auditorium in which laypeople sit mesmerized by the high-tech display of music, video, and drama, performed by a cadre of professional musicians and media technicians. The call to worship in such churches might well be given as, "We're glad you're here. Now sit back, relax, and watch us worship God for you." Good liturgy will always involve the people in the activity of worship.

## FOR THE BENEFIT OF OTHERS

The third response from Saliers's interviewees—that they did not understand what was happening in worship—gets at a third major component of good liturgy, which is that it should benefit the people. If worship by definition is the work of the people, then to invite worshipers to do something they do not understand will render the liturgy ineffective. Good liturgy can and should include an element of mystery, yet public worship must be structured to allow the people, all the people, to participate as fully as they choose.

One of the most common protests against liturgy is that it is simply "mindless ritual," the performance of rote actions that have no connection to the heart. That happens sometimes, of course. Yet in such cases, we can at least locate the problem accurately in the heart of the worshiper. When worship mystifies and confuses the participants, there's no way of telling what the people would do with it if they did understand it. Brad Berglund urges worship leaders to create "mindful ritual."[9] When planning worship, we ought to constantly imagine ourselves in the place of the worshiping congregation and ask, "Will they understand what this worship element is about?" and "How will this action facilitate their worship of God?" It is always the responsibility of the worshipers to open their hearts to God; no one can do that for them. Yet it is also true that "the prompters of worship, the leaders on the platform, have a responsibility to offer effective and varied avenues of worship so participants can respond in fresh ways."[10]

To undertake the task of planning worship is to go beyond the matter of people's experience. Experience is a most subjective measure; it is maddeningly unpredictable and is affected by the individual's temperament, preferences, and prior experience. Christian liturgy is "something prayed and something enacted not something thought about or merely 'experienced.'"[11] What people experience in worship is largely beyond our control as worship planners. But if the liturgy has been properly constructed, their ability to experience God will be greatly enhanced. To do so is our job as liturgists.

## RECOVERING GOOD LITURGY

Recovering our commitment to liturgy as the work of the people is the key to renewing worship in our churches. Our ability to produce healthy, vital churches where people are discipled and inspired to win others to Christ will be seriously undermined if worship is not properly focused. Far too many churches have, to use Marva Dawn's term, dethroned God by reducing the people's offering to God to something merely financial.[12]

Even more obvious today is the fact that many churches view music as the only way in which people can participate in worship. This produces a stunted and unhealthy liturgy that will not serve well for the long term. And the performance-oriented worship that is now so common is a significant factor in producing the pastoral burnout that plagues our clergy. To be asked, week in and week out, to produce the kind of religious show that will keep people coming back for more is a burden that even the most committed and talented pastors cannot bear for long.

Beyond the toll on our pastors is the toll that performance-oriented worship is taking on the church itself. Sally Morganthaler worries that "we are not producing worshipers in this country, rather, we are producing a generation of spectators, religious onlookers lacking, in many cases, any memory of a true encounter with God, the product of the tangible sense of God's presence and the supernatural relationship that our inmost spirits crave."[13] To be fair, the passivity of the modern worshiper is not solely the fault of worship planners, it is endemic to popular culture. And therein lies the first step in recovering good liturgy.

## FIGHTING CONSUMERISM

Modern culture is consumerist. This is the inevitable result of the "progress" that allows human beings to produce much more goods than they actually need. The surplus of production means that the people shopping for a new car, for example, can be choosy—they can demand discounts, rebates, or added service. The consumer always has the option of shopping elsewhere, which is why, as they say, the customer is king. Only the most naive pastor could believe that this consumerist attitude never shows up in church on Sunday. Because it does, pastors must always be prepared to point people away from themselves and towards God in worship. Otherwise, people will seldom progress beyond the point of test driving God to see if He meets their needs. Incredibly, many liturgies are designed without taking this phenomenon into account.

A byproduct of our consumer culture is passivity.[14] Overwhelmed by information, we adopt a passive attitude toward that information, mostly ignoring it. Much of the information we receive comes through the media and is aimed at inducing the purchase of some product. Neil Postman, among others, has suggested that people have learned to process this information without acting on it, purely as a survival skill. Imagine what would happen if we really did act on every advertisement we encountered for fast food. Our household budgets—to say nothing of our cholesterol counts—would be in serous trouble. So the ability to process information without acting on it can be a useful skill. But what happens when that same consumer skills walk into church on Sunday morning?

Knowledge is power, so good liturgists will keep this tendency for passivity among "consumers" of worship in mind when planning liturgy. Because people often prefer to be passive spectators of worship, good liturgists do not begin a service with an invitation to do nothing. A worship leader has, at best, three to five minutes at the beginning of a service to counteract the passive tendency of the worshiper. That is why some pastors make it an inviolable rule that the first musical offering must be something that *everyone* can sing. In a typical service, a group of highly skilled and well-trained musicians opens the service by performing for the people and then invites them to stand and join in. Have you observed the result? About 20 percent of the congregation will sing while the rest stands staring into space, growing more passive by the moment. It's over! Bad liturgy! Good liturgy does not allow worshipers to become spectators.

## DOING THEOLOGY

Good liturgy involves the congregation in more than simply taking action. It involves the people in thinking about God—in doing theology. Don Saliers captures the importance of this when he writes,

Liturgical worship begins and ends in praising, thanking, and blessing the reality of God. This is what some have called "theological-prima"—primary theology. Here is the revolutionary notion at the heart of liturgical theology, to pray to God is to be a theologian. Plus the gathered church at prayer is doing theology from which more abstract forms of critical reflection and "secondary theology" emerge.[15]

Many people think of theology as dry, boring, and hard to understand. Yet real theology fosters our relationship with God, just as worship, not coincidentally, is designed to do. The early church had a saying, *lex orandi, lex credendi*, which means "the rule of prayer is the rule of faith." All genuine theology is a reflection upon the worship of God and leads to orthodoxy—right praise. This is why worship must have theological integrity; it is the very heart of the church's proclamation of what it believes.

A commitment to creating good liturgy will lead pastors, worship leaders, and musicians to think reflectively about every aspect of the service to see how the participatory nature of worship is served by any particular element. This will have a profound effect on some of the most common aspects of worship. For example, when music is performed by professionals it may merely reinforce the consumerist thinking of worshipers, not lead them in offering their own praise to God.

Also, preachers must think liturgically about the place of the sermon. Robert Webber notes that because of the instructive nature of preaching, it is more likely to produce "cerebral overkill" than any other part of the service.[16] Preachers can unwittingly reinforce the passive tendency of their congregants through their preaching. As a teacher of preaching, I see that preaching is evolving to find its place within contemporary liturgy. It is unlikely to return again to the status it had in my boyhood church—where the preaching *was* the liturgy. This evolution of preaching will take some of the heat off pastors who have felt compelled to carry the entire liturgical load. It will also force preachers to craft sermons that follow the natural progression of the rest of the service. That will require good communication and planning by pastors, musicians, and everyone who has a part in shaping the liturgy. While sermons are necessarily becoming shorter, that trend need not undercut the quality of preaching nor its significance in our worship.

## MANAGING DIRECTION

Balancing the structure of worship means giving attention to the direction and flow of the liturgy. In his book *The Integrity of Worship*, Paul Hoon indicates various directions that worship may take—sometimes simultaneously. Among those he mentions are from God to the assembly, from the assembly to God, and from one to another within the assembly.[17] Each of these directions should be addressed by the liturgy— as should the whole person. Webber reminds us that "an authentic encounter with the living God in worship will touch the whole person— mind, emotions, and the symbolic and intuitive dimensions of the person."[18] Kneeling, a common practice in Catholic or Episcopal services, is seldom done in evangelical churches. Many of us could leave our bodies at home and still participate in a typical worship service.

## ELICITING RESPONSES

Robert Webber suggests several corporate responses that can be used during the service of the Word, which is what most evangelical churches employ most of the time. They provide a starting point for considering ways to increase the participation of the congregation in worship and hence point in the direction of "good liturgy."

First, the congregation can respond to the reading of Scripture. Ending the public reading of the Bible with the words "This is the Word of the Lord" followed by the congregational response "Thanks be to God!" is simple enough. Yet it both teaches people to honor Scripture and voices their commitment to the Word just read. Another response to the Word might be to sing the "Gloria" or a hymn or song that has Scripture as its theme.

Second, a congregation may respond with silence. This is a legitimate way for people to indicate submission, reverence, and most all, attentiveness to the Spirit of God. The wall-to-wall noise of so many modern services is not at all conducive to hearing God speak. Silence is particularly needed before prayer because "the congregation needs time to center itself corporately and individually."[19] I have conducted services devoted to silence, and it was amazing to sense how people responded to God, given the opportunity. Silence is not "dead air" in a worship service.

Another important way to call the people to participate in worship is through the use of specially chosen musical texts that clearly serve a liturgical purpose at some point in the order of worship. Whether the song illuminates Scripture, prepares the people to pray, to hear the Word, or to respond to it, music can be a powerful means of drawing people into the liturgy. At first, the worship leader may need to properly introduce these musical texts to insure that people grasp their importance. But after a short while, thoughtful worshipers will begin to look for such linkages in the liturgy.

Finally, creeds are a meaningful way to elicit a response to the Word from worshipers. The use of creeds dates to the early church but has fallen on some hard times lately due to the perception by some that they represent "empty ritual." Yet if repeating the Apostles' Creed—words that many have died for—is an empty act, the sad commentary is not upon the creed but upon us. Creedal statements abound in worship books and online. And any pastor can write a litany for his or her congregation that affirms faith by congregational response.

## PRAYING TOGETHER

Most congregations could do better at involving worshipers in prayer. While the pastoral prayer has a rightful place in our worship, the prayers of the people should be expressed as well. Instituting changes in this aspect of worship can be difficult depending on the congregation's history. One way to get members of the congregation involved in public prayer is to ask for volunteers ahead of time to be prepared to offer a brief prayer during the service.

## FREEDOM IN STRUCTURE

Although there are clear biblical guidelines for structuring worship, there are no fixed rules about what goes in or stays out of a worship liturgy. That there be some order or plan is imperative, but how that order is communicated is something individual pastors who know their own congregations best should determine. "The Apostle Paul did not mandate forms or liturgies to guide the Spirit's flow in the worship of his congregations, he simply urged Christians to exercise self-control out of consideration for others and for the reputation of the faith."[20] With this kind of freedom, no pastor should feel confined or overly limited by giving due attention to the liturgy. "St. Paul frequently reminds his converts that corporate worship requires an order that maintains a balance between the impulses of the individual and the needs of the group. A liturgy is simply whatever a community does to preserve a fruitful relationship between these things."[21] To construct good liturgy, pastors must constantly evaluate the liturgical life of their churches. Worship is the people's work. Giving them the tools for it and a structure in which to do it is a most caring and loving act by a pastor. Having good liturgy is always possible; having no liturgy is not an option.

## CHAPTER SIX

# TRADITION

## *Lessons from an Old Friend*

—⟋⟍⟋—

*To those who say that we cannot turn the clock back, the*
*answer is that when we need to, we do it every year. And*
*in the deeper case of the church of Christ, that setting*
*back of the clock means reformation and revival. To go*
*forward the church must always first go back.*
—Os Guinness

> **SILVER BULLET**
> Time-tested worship practices are invaluable aids for
> worship planners amid changing times.

*F*iddler on the Roof* has long been a favorite musical of mine, partly because of the insight it offers into human behavior. When Tevye, the peasant farmer, sings of tradition, he gets at the very heart of the Jewish culture of pre-revolutionary Russia. Every man, woman, boy, and girl in the village knows his or her place in life because of the traditions of their culture. The story deals with the testing and even the overthrow of some of those traditions; but even amid changing times, this band of Russian Jews is held together by common beliefs and practices. In the midst of a sea of social, political, and even religious upheaval, there are islands—such as the Sabbath—that keep the people anchored to their identity as God's people. That is the value of tradition.

The place of tradition was brought powerfully home to me several years ago on a visit to Israel. A popular poster there featured two items: a piece of ancient clay pottery and a clear glass beaker of the sort used in a chemistry lab. The caption read, "Israel's future is in her past." That is the essential role of tradition—not to bind and stifle progress but to serve as a chart and compass so that in the midst of relentless change, people can retain their collective identity. That is why tradition is essential for creating a well-founded liturgy.

## TRADITION VERSUS TRADITIONALISM

Unfortunately, *tradition* has become something of a dirty word in many contemporary churches. Some churches have thoughtlessly discarded any semblance of tradition because of a modern bias in favor of innovation. Based on the belief that the church must be relevant, many congregations have rid themselves of anything beyond a certain age—usually the age of the power-holders in the church. Tradition is a tempting target for those seeking to revitalize the worship of the church. And, the truth is, some traditions have far outlived their usefulness. But to become liturgically allergic to anything over twenty years old is both shortsighted and misinformed.

Sally Morganthaler argues that "we have failed to make an impact on contemporary culture not because we have not been relevant enough, but because we have not been real enough."[1] The problem that we face when dealing with stiff or meaningless worship forms is not tradition but *traditionalism*. Tradition is simply a record of how the church has typically interpreted Scripture, worshiped, and generally lived out the faith in the world around it. Traditionalism is the attitude, encountered sooner or later by every pastor, that says "we've never done it that way before." Those words—which some have aptly labeled the seven last words of the church—are the mantra of traditionalism and sound the death knell for authentic worship.

Traditionalism is always a danger, and, to be fair, it affects worship perhaps more than any other aspect of church life. Worship can easily fall into a rut that is deepened by years of passive acquiescence by a congregation. A pastor is more likely to successfully add command-ments to the stone tablets than to initiate changes to the order of worship at such a traditionalistic church. There is no doubt that traditionalism is a threat to the vitality of any church, particularly in its worship. Yet some knowledge of and respect for tradition is important for worship planning. Tradition is the friend, not the enemy, of good liturgy.

## TRADITION AS AN ANCHOR

Tradition is helpful for worship planners because it provides stability for a congregation. In his book *No Place for Truth*, David Wells comments on the importance of tradition:

> Tradition is the process whereby one generation inducts its suc-cessor into its accumulated wisdom, lore, and values. The fam-ily once served as the chief conduit for this transmission, but the family is now collapsing, not merely because of divorce but as a result of affluence and the innovations of a technological age . . . Film and television now provide the sorts of values that were once provided by the family. And public education . . . has also contracted out of this business, pleading that it has an obli-gation to be value-neutral. So it is that in the new civilization that is emerging, children are lifted away from the older values like anchorless boats on a rising tide.[2]

A glance at a daily paper or newscast underscores the validity of Wells's analysis. Since the church is one of the few surviving institu-tions where tradition can be transmitted, we would do well to think long and hard about the dismissal of any given tradition. That does not offer a free pass to *every* tradition or ensure that it will be useful in crafting worship in the future. Judgment, discernment, and a thorough knowledge of the congregational context must be employed when weighing the place of any tradition in the life of a church. The lack of just such a discerning approach has led to a vexing polarization over worship in many congregations.

## COMPETING FORCES

Tradition is helpful also because it helps to balance two competing forces that are now driving the debate over worship in the church. In his book *Beyond the Worship Wars*, Thomas Long suggests that "much of the confusion, uncertainty, and conflict over worship today is generated by the collision of two powerful forces—forces that have developed gradually in the American church over the past fifty years and they are now engaged in a struggle over the soul of the church's worship." He labels these the "Hippolytus force" and the "Willow Creek force."[3]

Hippolytus was an early Christian leader whose eucharistic prayer has been used to construct the most prominent forms of the worship services in both the Roman Catholic and most mainline Protestant churches. There is a predictable liturgical structure in all these churches, with some obvious denominational variations. The Hippolytus force is levied by ecclesiastical insiders, those who are believers and have a good deal of exposure to traditional worship. Not surprisingly, the Hippolytus force tends to create liturgy that positively mystifies many unchurched folk.

The Willow Creek force is named for the seeker-sensitive approach popularized by Willow Creek Community Church. This force drives toward making the worship service accessible to "unchurched Harry and Mary." Long observes that "what began as a strategy in evangelism, quickly became a movement in popular, casual, contemporary media-inspired worship."[4] Again unsurprisingly, seeker-sensitive worship tends to be viewed as shallow and unsatisfying by those who are accustomed to traditional liturgy. Ironically, seeker-sensitive worship has become so pervasive that it is now in danger of becoming traditional-istic. Many churches are trying to balance these forces by adopting a hybrid approach, employing aspects from both liturgical systems. (More on blended worship later in the book.)

Neither of these forces, in spite of the good they have offered, is adequate for shaping worship today. The Hippolytus force is too rooted in past forms of worship, while the Willow Creek approach abandons too much of the historically and theologically based wor-ship that has shaped the church for two millennia. It is, as someone observed, "a Young Life meeting for grownups,"[5] offering little depth for believers seeking to grow to maturity in Christ.

While there are clear problems with the Hippolytus approach (which we'll deal with in a later chapter), the primary pressing issue at this point in the life of the church is to recover the proper value of tradition. In a time when the velocity of change has a dizzying effect on church lead-ers and laypeople alike, it is vital to have some historic anchors that will enable the congregation to always know who they are and where they are in the faith. We have that much to gain from tradition.

## LEARNING FROM TRADITION

C. S. Lewis compared theology to a roadmap, a guide for navi-gating unfamiliar territory. Having a map of England is not the same thing as being in England; but if you were to go there, the map could prove extremely helpful. The map represents the cumulative experi-ence of many people who have been to England. It would be both foolish and arrogant to disparage the map as useless because it was old. In the same way, doing theology is not exactly the same thing as experiencing God. But as the record compiled by others who have experienced God, theology can be of great usefulness to those who want to explore the landscape of the faith.

In a similar fashion, Lewis's analogy applies to the worship tra-ditions of the church. Those traditions, in and of themselves, do not constitute the worship of God. But to the extent that they have stood the test of time as an accurate record of those who *have* experienced God in worship, they can be extremely useful to those of us who are orienting the worship of the church amid the changing landscape of modern and postmodern culture.

Worship books, often published by denominational presses, contain the basic approaches that the church has used for worship, the sacraments, and basic rituals such as weddings and funerals. These books are an invaluable liturgical reference for planners of worship not because we will adopt unthinkingly any given prayer, litany, or other piece of liturgy, but because they provide some parameters for what is clearly Christian worship. Every pastor would do well to own several such worship books.

Beyond the practical help provided by these sources, examining the traditions of the church has a way of deepening the reader's understanding of worship, which improves one's ability to plan services of greater depth and scope. Taking people deep with God is always a good idea. Anything that enables a pastor to do that is worth a second look. Learning from tradition will add dimensions to worship planning in at least six areas.

### SILENCE

Years ago, when I first began to try to fill in the gaps in my own liturgical understanding, I became aware of the almost total absence of silence in the worship services I was orchestrating. To be still before God is a common admonition in Scripture, yet it has almost no place in the worship life of many churches. Daniel Frankforter is painfully correct when he notes that "nothing characterizes the worship of American Protestants more than its avoidance of silence."[6] Many worship services seem to be running on caffeine or amphetamines—they are frenetically paced and can't seem to make themselves sit still or be quiet. Silence provides a moment when, as Marva Dawn writes, "we have to face ourselves, our cares, our ugliness, our emptiness. Most difficult of all, we might encounter God."[7] William Willimon asks,

"Are we afraid that in our silences God might come and surprise us? Is that why we keep talking, and moving, and singing?"[8]

This discipline has a long and effective history as an aid to worship, and we do well to help our people recover this ancient tradition in new forms. The emphasis here is upon teaching the church to learn the power of silence. To simply impose silence on a typical congregation would be the surest way to ensure a speedy pastoral vote. To institute this practice will require wisdom and tact.

## PASTORAL CARE

A study of the worship tradition of the church through the ages compared with contemporary evangelical worship will yield one glaring contrast. Whereas the typical modern service almost always takes an upbeat, celebratory tone, Christian worship throughout the centuries has been more balanced, reflecting the full spectrum of human experience. Our worship has become overly positive, one-dimensional, and boringly predictable.

One result of this shift is that worship now has difficulty functioning as a form of pastoral care. Every pastor realizes that on any given Sunday, his or her congregants present a bewildering array of issues, attitudes, and life circumstances. While no worship service could be expected to address all these disparate concerns, worshipers who are dealing with issues such as grief, divorce, or illness can tolerate a series of pep rallies for God only so long. This may be one factor for understanding the infamous back door of the church. When worship does not address the full spectrum of life experiences worshipers face, they simply leave.

The Christian worship tradition has always included the full dimension of human life in the liturgy. That is true because people bring a variety of problems to church with them each Sunday, and they all need to feel included in what is happening. Those who doubt or feel abandoned by God are not likely to respond well to a steady diet of upbeat praise songs and happy aphorisms. I have inwardly grimaced while leading worship when my eyes fell upon a person sitting in the congregation whom I knew to be dealing with some difficult issue and realized that the service I had constructed had no place for them to "lay their heads." Walter Brueggemann suggests that "the problem with a hymnody that focuses on equilibrium, coherence, and symmetry . . . is that it may deceive and cover over. Life is not like that. Life is also savagely marked by dis-equilibrium [and] incoherence."[9] Pastors who recognize this reality in the lives of their parishioners and find ways to address it will find their own ministerial effectiveness deepened and their credibility enhanced as people come to view them as priests in the best sense of that word.

## COMMUNION OF SAINTS

Beyond dealing with the immediate crises faced by worshipers, Christian liturgy has included expressions of sorrow and disappointment, because every worshiping congregation is part of the communion of saints. Our world is filled with people who are at any given moment experiencing tragedy, persecution, and despair. Don Saliers points out that "our lives and liturgies are incomplete until we learn solidarity with others who suffer and allow others to touch our suffering."[10] This concern for the plight of humanity is echoed loudly and clearly in the ultimate expression of the church's worship tradition, the Psalms. Some suggest that a full two-thirds are laments. Learning to express lamentation over human suffering is an aid to worship. Saliers writes,

Praise and thanksgiving grow empty when the truth about human rage over suffering and injustice is never uttered. Prayer may be sincere, and God may certainly be praised and glorified in the absence of acknowledging such a truth about human suffering, but the revelatory character of prayer, liturgical or devotional, is diminished when no laments are ever raised.[11]

Worship that does not express the full range of human experience will never be fully effective in bringing people into communion with

God. The traditions of the church, then, are an aid to true worship because they give full voice to human experience.

## CONFESSION

That it pays requisite attention to the realities of human life is one reason the Christian worship tradition has always included the confession of sin. Worshipers in evangelical churches seldom encounter a reference to confession and forgiveness in the liturgy. Yet human beings have a God-given need to confess sin and to know they are forgiven. The elaborate sacrificial system detailed in Leviticus was not created to provide community barbecues for the Israelites. It was instituted to meet the people's ongoing need to confess sin and find forgiveness. Don Saliers is surely correct when he says that "without acknowledgment of our sin and provision for experienced forgiveness, our prophecy is fruitless."[12]

Pastors find no greater joy in our priestly role than that of announcing God's forgiveness of those who earnestly seek Him. The puzzling question is why we do it so seldom. Surely it is not because we see our people as beyond sinning. Any pastor who pays attention to his or her congregation knows otherwise. Recovering the tradition of confession, albeit in a more contemporary form, could be a key to the renewal and revitalization of many churches. William Willimon writes, "We confess in order to express our acceptance of God's penetrating knowledge of us, our boldness (made bold because of God's love for us) to stand face to face with as much truth about ourselves as God's love enables us to bear."[13]

Traditionally, Christian worship has always been in touch with both the lives of its people and the essence of the gospel. Whether using traditional forms, adapting them in creative ways, or finding other means such as music, silence, or eucharistic invitations, regular acts of confession ought to find their place in our liturgical practices.

## THE CHRISTIAN YEAR

Perhaps the most valuable asset in the Christian worship tradition is the Christian calendar. I grew up in an ethnically mixed neighborhood in Tucson, Arizona. With the exception of the Lutherans across the street and the one non-churchgoing family down the block, everyone on that street was Roman Catholic. My family, which attended a conservative, revivalist church, was about as far from Roman Catholicism as it was possible to be. Nothing underscored that more than our absolute ignorance of the Christian year. When my Roman Catholic playmates talked about Lent or Advent, they might as well have been speaking Cantonese. I remained ignorant of this distinctly Christian way of marking time until I attended seminary. Sadly, many churches continue to ignore this rich tradition, and others are abandoning it as out of date.

Based on the life of Jesus, the Christian year begins with Advent, the fourth Sunday before Christmas, and takes the Christian community on an annual journey that gives expression to the full dimensions of human experience as modeled in the life of our Savior. As a pastor responsible for planning the worship services of the church, I finally grasped the incredible value of this aspect of Christian tradition. To be on the same "liturgical page" with thousands of other churches enabled me to tap a variety of resources, converse with others who were contemplating similar themes, and save precious time in the planning of worship. It is heartening to find more and more evangelical pastors awakening to the power and usefulness of this tradition. To keep step with rhythm of the Christian year—which sometimes parallels but often starkly contrasts with the way our world keeps time—is an important element of the church's identity and makes it possible to stay the course in the midst of rapid change. The Christian year is also an extremely useful tool for teaching children the rudiments of the faith and is a wonderful aid for helping young and old alike enter into worship.

## THE LECTIONARY

Closely related to the Christian year is the lectionary. Lectionaries are systematic approaches to Scripture reading not unlike the now popular one-year Bible reading programs. Robert Webber helpfully summarizes the value and structure of the lectionary:

> The structure of the Christian lectionary is very simple. (1) Scripture is organized into a three-year cycle of readings, known as years, A, B, and C; (2) each set of Sunday readings has an Old Testament lesson, an epistle, a Gospel, and a Psalm. All four scriptures reflect the theme of the day in the Christian Year.[14]

For pastors and worship planners, the immediate value of the lectionary is in the ability to plan far ahead. I once served as part-time pastor in a small, rural church. I also had a full-time job as a college professor, which made time a precious commodity. Even though most of the people in that country church had no idea what a lectionary was, I used it every week so I would always know where worship was headed and could use my limited time most effectively. The lectionary also helped me keep this little church "in time" with the rest of the Christian community, which helped them appreciate and value their place in the body of Christ.

Interestingly, long-term planning is becoming essential for churches that have adopted a contemporary approach to worship using elements such as drama and video presentations. This ancient tradition may become a boon to those who are trying to stay on the cutting edge of worship evolution.

## CONVERGENCE

The value of the lectionary to contemporary worship planners is one more reason why, liturgically speaking, "everything old is new again." Nowhere is this more true than in *convergent worship*. This approach attempts to combine the best of both worlds, fusing a post-modern approach to the Christian faith with elements of the Christian worship tradition that can be reinterpreted, adapted, or in some cases simply appropriated for contemporary use. Writers including Robert Webber in *The Young Evangelicals*, Leonard Sweet in *Postmodern Pilgrims*, and Brian McClaren in *A New Kind of Christian* and *The Church on the Other Side* offer a starting point for thinking about how tradition can enhance the worship life of the contemporary church. Robert Webber identifies six elements of worship that exhibit the convergence phenomenon:[15]

- Restored commitment to the sacraments, especially the Eucharist

- A desire to know more about the early church

- Stress upon the unity of the church and a desire to overcome division

- The embrace of diversity and enculturation

- Integration of form and freedom in worship

- An increased role for ritual, gesture, symbol, and visual art in worship

It's exciting to watch elements of the Christian liturgical tradition—acts and approaches that were formed centuries ago—finding new vitality among twenty-first-century congregations. Worship leaders are giving ancient liturgies and acts of worship modern and postmodern reinterpretations and are finding that these older practices possess the power to awaken the worship of God's people in any age.

Tradition is our friend, and even the busiest pastors can take some time to reacquaint themselves with the forms and practices that have served the church well over the centuries and to measure their work against the chart and compass of the Christian tradition.

## CHAPTER SEVEN

# RENEWAL

## *Embracing Change without Losing Focus*

—〰—

*Because the Holy Spirit cannot be controlled, spirited
worship is spontaneous and thus a point of vulnerability
for religious institutions. By definition, opening our lives
to God in worship has an uncontrollable quality to it.*

—Brad Berglund

### SILVER BULLET

By embracing, not fearing, worship renewal,
pastors free themselves to lead.

Like fiddlers on the roof, pastors seek to maintain balance as we scratch out the tune of worship each week. Tradition is our place to stand amid the unnerving pace of change. Apart from some link to the bigger story, all of us would soon become disoriented and disconnected by the strong currents of culture. It is tradition which anchors us.

But as Tevye himself discovered in the musical *Fiddler on the Roof,* tradition is not static. It must be constantly redefined and reinvested with new meaning if it is to remain timeless and help people stay connected to the bigger story. When Tevye allows his daughters to marry men of their own choosing rather than employing the services of the matchmaker, he does not discard Jewish tradition but finds a deeper, more inclusive aspect to it—the joy of human love and marriage—that will fit it for a new day. In the end, even the forced expulsion from their beloved village of Anatevka, the only place they have ever known, cannot prevent the family from holding on to the steadfast belief that God is watching over His people. Authentic tradition is evidenced precisely by its ability to be transferred from one generation to the next. But that transmission can be inexact, unpredictable, and, especially for the older generation, a painful and anxiety-ridden experience.

There is a transfer of tradition now taking place in the church, and it is producing its share of unpredictability and anxiety. The gospel must continually be translated into the lingua franca of culture. That is always difficult, but particularly so in today's postmodern world. Pastors constantly feel caught between the competing concerns for relevance but against accommodation, for tradition but against traditionalism. Yet as Brad Berglund reminds us, there is more to the dilemma than meets the eye. A new wind of the Spirit is blowing through the church, and one of its most obvious manifestations is the current renewal that is taking place in worship. This renewal is not to be uncritically embraced, but neither should it be feared. It is a welcome change, and it is here to stay.

## HERE TO STAY

I grew up in a conservative church within the revivalist tradition, where the sermon reigned supreme, trumped liturgically only by the altar call, or response to the proclaimed Word. Every other element of the service existed to serve these two aspects of worship in some way. But around the early 1970s, something began to change. With the Jesus Movement and with the Charismatic Renewal, a new wind began to blow through many churches. Because it was largely associated with Pentecostalism, this renewal was often resisted, reasoned away, or even demonized in evangelical churches. Yet this movement ultimately took hold in one aspect of mainstream American Christianity, and that was worship.

Today, worship renewal of some sort is taking place in nearly all Christian churches in North America. Some have embraced it wholeheartedly, even uncritically at times, falling into bizarre and untoward practices that cannot stand the scrutiny of the Christian tradition. Others have embraced worship renewal in ways that have reenergized their churches. Interestingly, a few others continue to resist renewal, holding tightly to the forms of worship they have always known and believing that the current renewal movement is a fad produced by modern culture.

Such thinking is mistaken. Notwithstanding the excesses that the movement has produced, it has breathed new life into the church and is here to stay. Going back to the way things were done in a previous generation is simply not an option. Thus, learning how to let go of the past and embrace the future of Holy Spirit–inspired worship is both justified and necessary.

## THE PROBLEM WITH THE PAST

In the previous chapter, we identified two competing forces that have influenced worship in North America throughout the past several decades. Thomas Long labeled them the Hippolytus force and the Willow Creek force.[1] The Hippolytus force describes the traditional worship practiced by a broad spectrum of Protestant churches, worship that relies on a regular form, pulpit-and-table-centered liturgies, and practices by congregations comprised mostly of insiders. The Willow Creek force is represented by the seeker-sensitive model in which worship is constructed with the aim of evangelizing those who have been disenchanted by the church. In the last chapter, a critique was leveled at the Willow Creek approach as being sometimes disconnected from the church's historic practices and liturgical heritage. Yet the Hippolytus force has produced problems of its own, for it has tended to create worship services that are disinviting of newcomers and can be boring even to insiders.

## DISINVITING

While visiting Australia I chose to worship in a large, city cathedral. Seated in that beautiful structure, surrounded by fantastic artwork, luminous stained glass, and rich Christian symbolism, the atmosphere was primed for worship. But a combination of bad acoustics, a lack of guidance from the leaders, and my own unfamiliarity with the church's liturgical approach left me feeling like a spectator. My mind roamed to other things because I was not really connected to the liturgy. The service was conducted for those in the know and left visitors like me feeling disinvited. This is a prime criticism of traditional approaches to worship: It is exclusionary.

Traditionalists tend to keep doing the same things, which *may* make sense to insiders but increasingly baffle and frustrate those who are new to or inquiring into the faith. Long argues that supporters of the Hippolytus force fail to see that "although Christian worship is a private event, it is done in a public place. The doors and windows of the church are figuratively always open and there is not authentic Christian worship without a genuine welcome and hospitality to the stranger."[2]

So the contention here is that whereas the Willow Creek force often drives worship too far in the direction of accommodating the outsider, the Hippolytus force has a tendency to ignore those who are not initiated into the faith. Newcomers simply don't get it and, therefore, cannot participate in what we do in church every Sunday. While that may be partly because of the sad state of religious knowledge in our culture, we must consider whether we will continue speaking to the average worshiper in what might as well be an unknown tongue. Was not Jesus' ability to meet people where they were and speak to them in words they could grasp central to His proclamation of the good news? How else could they be expected to make a reasoned decision about His claims to be Lord? Is not the originating characteristic of the Christian church, in its birth at Pentecost, the astounding discovery that the message of God was heard by everyone in his or her own language? Surely worship is intended to be inclusive, not exclusive. It is intended to call people to God, not repel them in frustration or anger.

## BOREDOM

The first problem with worship that is rooted too rigidly in traditional forms is that it can repel outsiders. A second problem is that it can bore insiders. As Long puts it,

the Hippolytus style of worship as actually practiced in most churches, is often, frankly, quite boring. You can plod along its once majestic path from gathering to blessing without much spirit, verve, or life. Sadly, the Sunday worship of many a traditional church has become something of a Chevy Bel Air: it starts every time and gets you safely from here to there, but the heart never races and the spine rarely tingles.[3]

It is painful for me to admit this because I love traditional liturgy; but the manner in which it is practiced by many churches will never attract new worshipers or even retain the existing ones. Letting go of outmoded attitudes and practices so as to allow the winds of revival to blow through the worship of a church is not the first step toward becoming an anything goes, Holy Roller society. It is simply a symbol of a congregation's decision to allow the Spirit to work within it, enabling its people to worship the Lord "in spirit and in truth." That is what people are longing to do, and there are ways to enable them to worship Him in creative new ways. That doesn't mean that we jettison all that has gone before. Tradition is a friend of the worship planner, an anchor and not deadweight. Yet we must be willing to allow the missional call of the church—and not "the way we've always done it"—to determine the structure of worship in the present age.

Sadly, in spite of much talk, the worship "renewal" in some churches amounts to a reshuffling of roles or rearranging of chancel furniture. Dan Kimball summarizes the frustration that has resulted in many within the church:

> Weekend worship services are becoming a definite issue for emerging generations. They wonder if coming together to worship really only consists of a few songs and a central focus on preaching. They feel more and more uncomfortable with the way many worship services profile one or two male-only leaders up front. They are wondering why there is hardly (if any at all) participation from the people in the congregation . . . They wonder why they can't have more freedom in worship to express to God their love and passion for him in ways that resonate with who they are.[4]

Having the courage to honestly face the issues Kimball and others raise about worship in the contemporary church will be the acid test of our commitment to listening to God's Spirit as He leads each local congregation, teaching them how to "sing to the Lord a new song." This will not be easy, especially for pastors, but that it is necessary to the future health of the church is beyond dispute.

## MARKERS OF RENEWAL

Leonard Sweet, among others, has written about an authentic approach to worship that he describes with the acronym EPIC, meaning experiential, participatory, image-based, and connecting.[5] One would do well to give attention to these categories in learning how traditional approaches to worship may need to change in the new century.

### EXPERIENTIAL

One of the most obvious characteristics of worship renewal is its emphasis on experiencing God. There are some notable cautions concerning looking at the phenomenon of human experience in worship (see chapter 3), yet there is no diminishing the importance people now place on relating to God through worship. People are unwilling to simply put in their time at a worship service that affords them no avenue to connect intimately with God. This means worship planners must intentionally move away from the didactic, or learning-centered, approach that has characterized so much of Protestant worship. This approach, which results in the pulpit-driven worship that character-ized the services of my boyhood church, seems predicated on the notion that everything people need spiritually can be taught to them through the sermon or some other form of teaching. As one who teaches preaching, I have no desire to dismiss the sermon as useless and outdated. But the point remains: We must deliver other ways for people to learn about the life of the soul. That is the primary value of contemporary worship music—it is experiential in its core. Regardless of its limitations (more on that in a later chapter), this music has clearly tapped the need in people to relate worship to their own experience.

## PARTICIPATORY

Worship is also moving at warp speed in the direction of partici-pation. Given the notion of liturgy as the work of the people, this is a healthy move and should be applauded. This shift is part of a larger movement toward congregationalism in all areas of church life, something that has caught the attention of church analysts around the world. This movement is seen in the increased call for the participa-tion of women as priests in Roman Catholicism and some Protestant churches and in the pervasive insistence for more lay involvement in all church ministries. This is a signal of a broad movement within church culture that will not be going away.

All evidence points to the fact that people are leaving churches where they feel shut out; therefore, it is essential for worship planners to find ways to include laypeople in the acts of worship. This under-scores the importance of sound liturgical thinking in the truest sense of the word. Make no mistake; this shift is likely to change the look of public worship in radical ways. That may be challenging for insiders to accept, but the alternatives are far less inviting.

## IMAGE-BASED

A third marker of worship renewal is the shift toward image-based worship. This is due, in part, to the influence of the media culture upon the church. Like it or not, motion pictures are the novels of our time. And whereas members of the Woodstock generation at first found music videos to be strange and unnecessary, their children see them as a natural and necessary extension of the creative expression of music. Let pastors with ears to hear, hear. Or better yet, let us develop eyes to see. The visual starvation of worshipers with plain meeting rooms is one reason so many evangelicals have joined the procession on the so-called Canterbury trail into Anglicanism—and some into Eastern Orthodoxy. Good liturgy is holistic; therefore, it must be visual as well as aural.

One caution should be voiced at this point. Worship planners should beware going overboard in using technology as a tool for reaching the media-savvy generation. Younger people are so immersed in media that they have effectively learned to ignore it. Baby boomers are often mystified by the ability of their children to study with music playing in the background. In fact, many are unable to concentrate without it. While parents find the "noise" impossible to ignore, their children do so without effort. One study done for churches that were deciding whether or not to invest money in video technology concluded the technological fireworks were essentially ignored by younger people while completely captivating the older generation. Let the buyer beware. The important factor in crafting image-conscious worship is not the amount of money spent or technology acquired but the ability to create balance between what is seen and what is heard.

## CONNECTIONAL

Finally, worship is becoming more connectional, meaning that it connects people together in an experience of vital community. Alienation and loneliness are two demons that are fueled by popular culture. Churches must find a way of enabling strangers to come together and find solidarity as the body of Christ. Among other things, this entails building church life beyond the hour or so of public worship. Sociologist Peter Berger contends that "minority viewpoints," such as the Christian faith, cannot sustain their knowledge claims alone. Only as they find significant relationships within a *cognitive minority* can they withstand the pressures of the majority culture.

This is powerfully demonstrated by the Christians of Australia. Although similar in some ways to American culture, Australia is a much more thoroughly secular society. The Australian church is clearly a cognitive minority. On my visit to Australia in the 1990s, I noticed the emphasis that Australian Christians place on fellowship and on building relationships between believers. They truly need one another. I have never been in an Australian church where people didn't stay after the service to have tea and just spend time with each other. The mad dash for the parking lot accompanies that the close of worship in many American churches would be out of place in that culture.

In fact, American culture is becoming more like Australian culture in the way it perceives the Christian faith. That makes it even more vital for Christians to develop relationships with one another. We need each other. This is why connecting people meaningfully to one another is a crucial element of worship.

## FAMILIAR LANDMARKS

Worship renewal is not only here to stay but is also rapidly accelerating. Liturgically speaking, "this is not your father's Oldsmobile." The pace of change tends to make the passengers—those of us within the church—nervous, so it's helpful to know exactly from where the changes are coming and where they are leading. Robert Webber has done an incredible service to the evangelical church by identifying eight common elements of worship renewal. These are the familiar landmarks that will help worship planners maintain stability while adapting worship in new and creative ways.

1. Worship renewal draws from biblical resources. Renewal is occupied with the question "How does the God who acted in the past act now in our worship?"

2. Worship renewal is characterized by an interest in the worship traditions of the past. We move into the future on the basis of the past, particularly the first five centuries of the church's worship understanding and practice.

3. Worship renewal generates a new focus on Sunday worship. Since Sunday worship is the pinnacle event of the church week, pastors and congregations are awakening to the need to bring new life to it.

4. There has been a virtual explosion of new music associated with the worship renewal movement, which views music as providing the "emotional substance of worship." Gaining prominence is an eclectic use of music that draws from ancient hymns, Scripture songs, chants, and gospel and contemporary songs.

5. Renewalists have an interest in restoring the arts to their rightful place in worship. Protestantism's historic rejection of visually based communication in favor of a verbal approach is beginning to be amended.

6. Worship renewal recognizes that worship is a celebration of the mighty deeds of God's salvation. This has caused a recovery of the service of the Christian calendar.

7. The role of the sacraments is taking on increased significance in the life of the church.

8. The renewal movement relates worship to the ministries of the church. For example, there is a recovery of the ministerial offices (including healing) that enable the people of God to reach out to others in a ministry of reconciliation. In other words, worship sets the agenda for the church's mission into the world.[6]

Nothing within Webber's list of foci within worship renewal appears to be revolutionary. And it is not difficult to imagine that any of these elements could be used in a given local church. The extent to which each is incorporated into any local church requires pastoral thoughtfulness and some skill at initiating change, but the potential reward of revitalized worship is more than enough incentive to try.

Ultimately, a church's embrace or denial of worship renewal will hinge on the pastor's and congregation's willingness to open their lives to God's Spirit. The Spirit seems to be moving a host of churches into a new, revitalized kind of worship. Opening ourselves to this movement is important for both the health of the church and the viability of the church's mission in a changing world. Brian McClaren caught the optimism of worship renewal when he wrote, "The way we traditionally expressed Christianity may be in trouble, but the future may hold new expressions of the Christian faith every bit as effective, faithful, meaningful, and world-transforming as those we've known so far."[7]

Given the faithfulness of the Holy Spirit to renew and guide the church through the centuries, we can confidently believe that our churches will find these "new expressions of the Christian faith" for our time and for the years to come.

## CHAPTER EIGHT

# MUSIC

## *Finding Common Ground*

—⟋⟍⟋—

*Music is the nuclear reactor of congregational worship. It is where much of the radioactive material is stored, where a good bit of the energy is generated and, alas, where congregational meltdown is most likely to occur.*
—Thomas Long

### SILVER BULLET
Pastors can effectively lead the music ministry of the church regardless of their own musical ability.

"When Satan fell from heaven, he landed in the choir loft and has resided there ever since." I don't know where that statement originated, but I know that it is an accurate depiction of the role of music in many congregations. What is it about music that gets people so riled up? For certain, it has nothing to do with musical ability. Some people who couldn't carry a tune in a bucket will do a fair imitation of Mount St. Helens over something the organist or the choir director did during a worship service. If you want to pick a fight with nearly anyone, just tell him the music he likes isn't any good. Everyone, it seems, has strong opinions about music.

Perhaps that's because music has been a significant factor in nearly everyone's spiritual formation. I admit that when I hear a piece of music from my childhood church days, perhaps something I haven't heard for years, the experience invariably brings back powerful memories and feelings—sometimes good and sometimes bad. Music has the power to evoke strong emotions. But the role of music in worship goes far beyond being a simple memory book designed to whisk us away on a nostalgic journey. If we are to lead a congregation of people in worship, all of whom will have some opinion about the role of music, we must understand its deeper purpose in worship and how we can properly utilize this marvelous gift from God to facilitate the praise of His people. First, we need to know why we sing.

## WHY CHRISTIANS SING

Praise the LORD!
Sing to the LORD a new song,
    his praise in the assembly of the faithful!
Let Israel be glad in his Maker,
    let the sons of Zion rejoice in their King!
Let them praise his name with dancing,
    making melody to him with timbrel and lyre!
For the LORD takes pleasure in his people;
    he adorns the humble with victory.
Let the faithful exult in glory;
    let them sing for joy on their couches
               —Psalm 149:1–5 RSV

God is a lover of music. Over and over in Scripture, the people of God are invited, yea commanded, to lift their voices in song to the Creator. That is why music has played a crucial role in the worship of both Israel and of the Christian church wherever it has taken root in this world.

## EXPERIENCE

The late Joseph Cardinal Bernardin observed that "What we do in liturgy is too vast and too deep to be left to our speaking voices. We need music so that we can fully express what we are about."[1] Any student of history knows the human race figured this out long ago. Every culture has had its way of expressing musically what it feels most deeply. The music may be tonal or some form of primitive chant, but in every culture it testifies that there are some human experiences that are too deep to be merely spoken. Liturgical scholar, James White underscores this fact:

> One of the reasons music aids worship is that music is a more expressive medium than ordinary speech. Music enables us to express an intensity of feeling through variety in speed, pitch, volume, melody, harmony, and rhythm. Thus, one has a greater range for expressiveness when singing than when speaking. Music can, and often does, convey a greater intensity of feeling than would be expressed in its absence.[2]

Because good liturgy is holistic—involving mind, body, and will—music is perhaps the best medium available for worship, for music involves all three necessary elements of human experience. When we give ourselves to singing, our mind, body, and will are engaged in a way that is rarely experienced otherwise.

## FELLOWSHIP

Beyond the manner in which music engages us, there is an important theological or liturgical component at work when Christians sing together. In *Life Together*, Dietrich Bonhoeffer attempted to plumb the depths of Christian fellowship. Not surprisingly, he turned his attention to the song of the church.

Why do Christians sing when they are together? The reason is quite simply because in singing together it is possible for them to speak and pray the same word at the same time. In other words, because here they can unite in the Word. All devotion, all attention should be concentrated in the Word in the end. The fact that we do not speak it, but sing it, only expresses the fact that our spoken words are inadequate to express what we want to say, but the burden of our song goes far beyond human words. Yet we do not hum a melody, we sing words of praise to God, words of thanksgiving, confession and prayer. Thus, the music is completely the servant of the Word, it elucidates the Word in its mystery.[3]

Bonhoeffer correctly sees the power of music to edify the body and the evidence that it gives of *koinonia*, or fellowship. Christians sing together to most appropriately express the depths of their praise and devotion as well as to demonstrate in a visible and aural way the unity of the body of Christ. Note how careful he is to underscore the subservience of music to the Word. This will be an important principle as we construct a theology of music in worship.

## DISCIPLESHIP

Listening to the music a congregation sings can be a window into the life of that particular church. Joseph Sittler wrote that "the songs the church sings are a lyrical way of disclosing what the faith knows and how we know."[4] This not only demonstrates the power of music to reveal a people's faith but also recalls the power of music to shape and inform faith.

Music clearly has a teaching, even a discipling, function to it. Church music has long been used to convey information through a text. Most of us who were raised in the church have hymn lyrics buried deep in our memories, phrases of theology and doxology that were planted there by singing the words over and over again. Indeed, part of the genius of early hymn writers, such as Isaac Watts and especially the Wesley brothers, was the ability to embed theological content into the minds of people who were unable to read. One reason churches should not dispense with good hymns, despite the fact that they are musically out of fashion, is that they represent some of the best theological content the church has produced. Obviously, the manner in which they are presented to the MTV generation will have to be carefully considered. Yet to discard these amazing lyrics simply because they do not match the current musical style would be a tragedy for this and future generations in the church.

## UTILITY

Church music also has a utilitarian function. To use Calvin Johansson's words, "Music's purpose here is to 'service the assembly.'"[5] Just how much we lean on music in the Christian assembly becomes evident when attending a wedding or funeral involving unbelievers. Often, these folk will have no musical agenda for the service, opting for a barebones reading of the ritual. The contrast between these services and even the simplest of Christian ceremonies is telling. We take the role of music in Christian worship too much for granted.

Typically, we enter into worship musically via preludes; we hear offertories and postludes as well. More often than not, we sing our praise to God. Music tends to be the first choice to cover almost any liturgical action, and it powerfully contributes to setting the mood for worship in the congregation.

## OFFERING

Beyond this, church music is itself an offering. From the beginnings of Israel's worship, to sing to the Lord has been considered an act of offering oneself to Him. One wonders how clearly modern worshipers grasp this fact. To bring one's heart, mind, and will together in a song of praise to God is every bit as real an offering as bringing a lamb, dove, or basket of firstfruits. How can this be? How can mere words have the same value as something tangible, such as an animal sacrifice? Remember that God doesn't need any material thing from us. What He really wants is the devotion of our whole lives. That offering can be symbolized as effectively by the joining of heart and voice as through material means—perhaps more so. Calvin Johansson declares that "music ministry is at its best a cooperative venture among congregation, pastor, and musicians. When these three are working together, the end result is a dynamic spirituality, seldom achieved in any other way."[6]

When this working harmony is not achieved, however, the result can be something just short of mortal combat. The easiest party to overlook in this liturgical trinity is the congregation. Musicians, especially church musicians, are often strong personalities who have a clear idea of what they hope to accomplish musically. Pastors also tend to have a clear idea of what they hope to see happen in the worship service, so there can be tension between the two parties. Too often the silent partner in this struggle for dominance is the congregation. Yet the congregation ought always to be the focal point of music ministry. The primary reason for using music in public worship is to facilitate the worship of the people. Therefore, all church music must be attuned to the congregation.[7]

This means that pastors and musicians have to choose music not according to their tastes or desires but based upon the congregation's ability to benefit from it. I've lost count of the number of worship services I've attended in which a talented musician failed to notice that the congregation was not following the music he or she was "leading." In some cases it was because they didn't know the music; in other cases it was because the selection was beyond their musical ability. Either way, it created bad liturgy. Pastors must remain engaged in music ministry precisely to ensure that it benefits the very people whom it is intended to serve—the congregation.

## TRANSFORMATION

When we worship God for who He is and what He has done, worship will prove transforming. Thus, the use of music in worship ought to be transformational. It ought to facilitate the discipleship and maturation of people in the faith. Liturgical music that merely entertains the crowd or showcases the skill of the musicians falls short of its intended purpose. Marva Dawn suggests that good church music should meet three criteria. It should (1) have God as the subject and object; (2) form the believer's character; and (3) form the Christian community.[8]

Dawn's first criterion may be too stringent. Testimony to one's personal experience is an established part of the hymnody in Christian tradition, and it often enhances worship. However, much of the Christian music written over the past one hundred years overemphasizes human experience rather than divine work. Pastors would do well to insist that the first piece of congregational music in a public worship service must have God as its subject and object. Worship is about God, not about my experience of God.

The second and third principles regarding the believer's character and the formation or edification of the community, seem inarguable. What is the point of using music that does not build up one's faith and the community? The fact that so few churches currently use music in a way that serves all three of these principles tells us that music can easily become a problem in worship.

## PROBLEM POINTS FOR CHURCH MUSIC

Music becomes a convenient whipping boy in the worship of the church when other things are going poorly. Samuel Adler laments the fact that "the music of worship has been cast in the role of convenient scapegoat for all maladies afflicting the attendance at, participation in, and comprehension of the worship service."[9] Yet there are legitimate reasons why church music has become problematic.

## THE PASTOR-MUSICIAN DYNAMIC

In the musical *Oklahoma*, there's a song that says, "The cowboys and the farmers should be friends." Like those two constant antagonists, pastors and church musicians should have enough common interests to ensure their harmony but often find themselves at odds. There are reasons for that. Many of my faculty colleagues who are musicians lament the general ignorance of pastors about music. Some pastors have the great fortune of being talented musicians, but many others, myself among them, have little musical ability. Most modern courses on worship recognize the need for prospective ministers to understand the spiritual ramifications of church music. Beyond their formative training, pastors need to continually broaden their grasp of methodology in music ministry.

On the other hand, pastors and musicians can be in total agreement regarding spiritual goals for the church but experience turmoil in terms of how those goals should be met musically.[10] As a former pastor, I freely confess my bias here toward the authority of the pastor. Yet I have noticed that when selecting music, musicians are often guided by the availability of musical resources and the pieces' general appeal. Unless the musician is particularly sensitive or is encouraged by an interested pastor, the church's music ministry can become thoroughly pragmatic, driven by the questions "What works?" and "What can we do?" While there are many talented musicians at work in our churches, the number of those who understand the *ministry* of music is far smaller. To effectively lead the congregation in worshiping through music is why the cowboys and the farmers—er, the pastor and the worship leader—should be friends.

## CONSUMERIST ATTITUDES

The narcissistic and consumerist culture has found its way into the church. In fact, it has found its way into the choir, the worship band, and even the pews, folding chairs, or theater seats of the congregation. While the role personal experience plays in this generation's worship is understandable, it is also fraught with problems. As one put it,

To hear the demand for 'music that speaks to me' is a rather telling phrase. It is first of all an indication of the importance we place upon self. Second, the phrase 'music which speaks to me' practically means, 'music that I like.' Musical pleasure, 'my' musical pleasure, becomes the criterion by which the church's music is judged.[11]

Everyone has musical preferences, and it is understandable that we will opt for music that moves us when given the choice. But to allow such subjective concerns to dominate the music ministry of the church is to condemn the congregation to a diet of spiritual baby food for life. Just as people need to be challenged by the Word of God in preaching rather than simply being reassured by what they already know and like best, congregations need also to be challenged from time to time to pursue personal and corporate growth in their worship experiences. What moves me musically doesn't necessarily move anyone else—and vice versa.

Of course it is possible to gather a group of people that is so thoroughly homogeneous that their viewpoints on liturgy, music, and the interpretation of Scripture are perfectly matched. But is that a church? The glory of the church, according to 1 Corinthians 12, is the unity it maintains without disavowing its diversity. Surely that has implications for the music ministry of any local church. Congregations that are uniform and predictable musically may need to ask themselves some rather basic ecclesiological questions. Most churches have to work continually on the issue of expanding their musical boundaries. Their willingness to do so is not an admission of failure or immaturity but a confession that they desire to take their calling to be a healthy community of faith seriously. Lest anyone think this musical temptation is new, a direct side-effect of modern and post-modern culture, read what Augustine wrote about music in the fifth century.

I vacillate between the risks posed by pleasure and the acceptability of enjoying things that promote well-being. But I am inclined rather to approve the use of singing in the church so that weaker minds through oral pleasures can be helped to worship. But whenever I realize that I am affected more by the quality of the voice than by the words being sung, I know that I have sinned greatly, and I wish there had been no music to hear (Confessions, 10:33).

At a minimum, we who lead worship must understand power of music for good and for ill. Music can easily become manipulative, particularly in a religious environment. When teaching worship I often show clips from popular movies first without the musical soundtracks and then with the music as intended. Music sets the stage, builds anticipation, triggers excitement, and plays on emotions. While we clearly want heartfelt music in our worship services, music can be used to manipulate responses, and that is always dangerous. Caution should be used, for example, when using music as a backdrop for prayer. What happens when we need to pray and there is no music available? Music can be a powerful ally in the hands of a sensitive and caring worship leader, or it can be reduced to a manipulative tool that substitutes human emotion for the genuine work of God's Spirit.

## NARROW TASTES

Given the fact that almost everyone, including entire congregations, has strong musical preferences, how are we to overcome musical parochialism in order to stretch ourselves in worship? This is a difficult problem for most pastors and church musicians. To meddle with the musical repertoire of a congregation is to pick a fight. Robb Redman correctly observes that "like a still pool, the real depth of attachment to existing musical and liturgical styles is discovered only when it is disturbed."[12]

In many congregations, particular musical selections are overused, regardless of their liturgical significance or appropriateness. I remember with horror a Sunday morning early in one Lenten season when a family visited our church and managed, somehow, to be asked to contribute the "special music" that day. As I listened to them deliver a song traditionally used on Easter Sunday, regaling the congregation with their expert harmony, I realized how inappropriate the music was for the day. That the musicians were highly skilled did not matter: A resurrection song simply did not fit with the Lenten theme of the day. The music had been chosen because it was a familiar and beloved song, not because it would enhance the worship of the church. The musical tail must not be allowed to wag the liturgical dog, and it is typically the pastor who must be in charge of the leash.

A significant amount of research argues that the musical tastes of human beings are set rather early in life.[13] That brings a sobering conclusion to worship planners. Regardless of how cleverly we may introduce the subject, the current generation of people under age fifty simply will not grow into lovers of classical music if they have not learned to enjoy it already. It is true that the older people grow the more open they tend to be toward different musical genres and the more complexity there is in their choices. But the fact remains that musical tastes, once formed, are long lasting.[14] This is a fact of life that pastors and church musicians must learn to accept. That doesn't necessarily mean we should abandon pipe organs and discard hymnals. But it does mean, as the church always has, that we must find ways to use music for its theological and liturgical purpose and not merely to satisfy musical tastes—ours or others'.

Consider what may happen when the current generation of baby boomers, who mostly control church music these days, must cede control of worship to another generation whose musical tastes are different from their own. Who knows what music may be used in the future as a "new song" is raised in praise to our God?

The bottom line in resolving the issue of musical preferences is that the ministry of music must be made to serve to the ecclesiological call of the church. Wren states that "theologically, we preach acceptance and inclusiveness. [But] musically, we proclaim rejection and exclusion on the culturally conditioned belief that 'good taste is more pleasing to God than bad taste.'"[15]

It's worth noting that Brian Wren is a classically trained musician and one of the preeminent hymn writers of our day. Even though his musical tastes would have been hardwired differently from those of many younger believers, Wren sees the broader ecclesiological picture that must leaven the musical ministry of modern congregations. Most churches enjoy music within a rather narrow band of styles, and most will need to broaden their musical practices in order to minister authentically with music. The pursuit of excellence and not the preservation of a particular style is the more worthy pursuit of music ministries.

And growth is possible. Musical cretin that I am, I have come to genuinely appreciate opera, among other types of music that were once foreign to me. Even people with narrowly defined musical preferences can come to appreciate music ministry that is offered in authentic devotion to God by those who give their all to make an offering pleasing to God and edifying to the congregation.

## TOWARD GOOD MUSIC

Much of the current turmoil in church music centers on the idea of aesthetics, or musical value. Critics of contemporary music argue that the music used to worship the Creator of the universe ought to be "good" music. The underlying premise is that music can be evaluated according to some standard that will gauge its appropriateness for use in worship. This is an aspect of music ministry that calls for careful reflection by pastors and worship leaders. In an earlier chapter, I introduced the influence of relativism in the church's worship. Musically, relativism manifests itself as the belief that there is no means other than subjective experience to gauge the value of worship music. Relativism says, "If you like it, it's good music—at least for you." Yet if we are serious about the church's call to worship and, beyond that, to be the church in a world captured by relativism, we'll need to move beyond "I like it" as the primary rationale for music selection.

A colleague related teaching aesthetics to a group of younger students. Holding up a music CD, he asked the class to tell what it would mean for him to say that this particular recording was good. Students responded predictably by saying, "It means you like it," and other subjective evaluations. Eventually other comments emerged, such as "It means this is well done" and "The lyrics are honest." The exercise demonstrated to young people, who often cite the relativistic canons of popular culture chapter and verse, that they themselves, when reflective, knew there are objective as well as subjective categories for evaluating music. This is important. For while we can allow that a broad range of musical styles may be of value in the church, it is undeniably true that not *all* music is worthy of inclusion in worship.

Thomas Aquinas wrote extensively in the area of aesthetics and suggested that the criteria of unity, clarity, and proportionality should be applied in assessing the aesthetic value of any piece of art or music. While Aquinas is heavily weighted toward Greek ideas of harmony and would likely frown on many modern, even modern classical, compositions that employ dissonance, his basic argument has value — namely that there are objective means for evaluating the appropriateness of any musical selection. Marva Dawns adds that "musical style in worship is not simply a matter of taste, what we do or don't like; rather it involves the appropriateness of a particular sound for the message expressed. If it becomes only an issue of taste, then power wins."[16] That is precisely where many churches are in terms of music ministry: Whoever has the power wins the worship war.

That word *appropriateness* is particularly helpful, for we need to think carefully about the propriety of any musical selection for worship. We are asking "Does it fit?" In the same way that the triumphant resurrection song did not fit a Lenten liturgy, many musical selections should be rejected based on their propriety for the occasion of worship. As an example, consider rock music. As a child of the 1960s, I enjoy rock music and own an extensive collection of it. Yet

I've not found that many biblical and theological themes are well served by that musical style. While there might be some exceptions, I don't see that hard rock music is appropriate for what typically happens in worship. That could change, however, as creative musicians compose pieces that effectively communicate energy, power, triumph, or other themes appropriate for worship.

One reason we give such care to musical selection is that music witnesses loudly and clearly to all around us, and we must be concerned with the content of that musical witness. Johansson reminds us that "integrity, truth, creativity, purity, economy, and self-denial rather than the traits of showmanship, pleasure, banality, cheapness, and amusement are suitable to church music."[17]

While there is certainly room for differing preferences and many musical styles will find their place in public worship, worship planners cannot afford to abandon the selection of music to the subjective tastes of musicians, the congregation, or even themselves. There are criteria for the selection of "good" music. Unity, clarity, proportionality, propriety, and, I would add, witness should guide our selection.

## THE PROBLEMS AND PROMISE OF CONTEMPORARY MUSIC

Perhaps more than any other element, music has fired the worship renewal that began in the late 1960s and continues in various forms today. The Holy Spirit himself moved upon preachers, musicians, artists, liturgists, and others to create a wave of new interest in and commitment to the worship of God. There is a new vibrancy and energy running through the worship of the church, largely due the increased participation of people in the liturgy, most evident in music and singing. I believe this movement continues to have great promise as it seeks to honor God and to edify the church in worship. But, like all great change movements, there are issues of concern that should be addressed.

## CONFUSING CATEGORIES

I confess that I dislike the term *contemporary*. Contemporary with what? I always wonder. And who determines what is contemporary and what is *traditional*? Ultimately, history will show that which was purely contemporary and that which endures. One of the reasons we're still singing "A Mighty Fortress is Our God" is that it was written in a way and at a level that transcends the times; it still communicates powerfully, both musically and textually. One supposes that there were lots of mediocre and downright awful songs composed around the time Martin Luther penned "A Mighty Fortress." Happily, they have not survived. I like to think of that whenever I'm subjected to some mindless ditty that will have the liturgical shelf life of a raw oyster. Meanwhile there are other "contemporary" pieces that will rightfully take their place alongside the "classics" in the church's repertoire.

Worship planners would do well to avoid the use of such confusing terms as *traditional, contemporary,* and *classic,* and select music based on its usefulness—not its age—in leading God's people in worship.

## MUSICAL AND LITURGICAL BALANCE

One of the most obvious clues that a church has "gone contemporary" in its worship is that it has adopted what Robert Webber calls a twofold pattern in worship. The first part of the worship consists of singing, the second part is preaching.[18] Having been raised in a church that had what I've called a tripartite pattern of worship, this shift doesn't seem alarming at first. Yet it is a radical change, given the liturgical history of the church. Webber points out that "in the past, Catholics made the Eucharist the primary communicator of grace, while Protestants made preaching the primary communicator of grace. The contemporary church makes *music* the primary communicator of grace."[19]

I've had the privilege of worshiping with a large number of different congregations and can attest to the accuracy of Webber's comment. In many churches, the service is dominated by the musicians. After singing for an extended period, the people are so exhausted emotionally — and physically — that nothing else commands much attention. The service is out of balance. One reason for adopting the fourfold movement in worship (see chapter 11) is that it maintains liturgical balance.

Beyond that imbalance it can create, the kind of music used in many churches today can actually discourage people from singing. Composer Brian Wren notes that

> Popular music today is soloistic; popular songs are not generally geared to audience participation; live music is no longer the norm, so our role as listeners is reinforced. Studio sound has become normative; the result is "electronic discouragement" because the quality of the pre-recorded sound persuades us that our own voices have little value.[20]

If no one in the congregation is singing, it doesn't matter how good the worship band is. Musicians must take great care to keep the congregation clearly in focus as service music is chosen.

This applies to the content of music as well. That old gag that defines a praise song as four words, three chords, and two hours may be an exaggeration, but it does make a point. Many newer songs are repetitive, both musically and textually. By repeating the same phrases over and over, worship leaders are often aiming for an emotional experience at the expense of engaging the mind. While there is room for that in worship, the temptation to employ music based purely on its emotional appeal should be resisted. It is true that simple, repetitive songs are easily learned by those who cannot read music — now an overwhelming majority of worshipers. That concern is not to be discounted. Yet there must be a way to balance the musical diet of worshipers with songs that offer richer content than that offered by many of today's songwriters.

Happily, there has been a shift in the past few years toward greater depth and musicality among songwriters. Yet there remains a shortage of current music that treats such significant themes as the Trinity, Scripture, justice, and compassion for the poor. In the meantime, many older hymns and songs can still be used effectively with modern worshipers.

## AMPLIFICATION

As a maturing flower child, I have fond memories of standing near the front at rock concerts where the music was so loud you couldn't hear yourself scream. I have more recent memories of such painful over-amplification during worship services. I attended a service recently at which the music was so loud you couldn't hear yourself sing. Not surprisingly, no one did. When the music is too loud, the congregation becomes passive and simply watches the performance by those holding microphones. The tendency toward passivity in worship is already too great. One way for worship leaders to counter this trend is to simply turn down the volume. Yet that is counterintuitive advice to most of today's musicians. Brian Wren suggests the reason:

> Most popular music today is delivered through high amplification. Audiences expect a thumping, throbbing, enveloping, sometimes ear-damaging sound . . . instrumentalist often crank up the volume unnecessarily and diminish their personal connection with the congregation . . . the sound is bigger than life and the person who makes it is regarded as bigger than life . . . Few singers of popular music know how to enable group singing, because their training, skills, and disposition are focused on performance.[21]

There is no going back to acoustic worship, at least not for larger groups. Amplification is a useful and necessary factor in worship. Yet far beyond helping people to hear and understand the text of music, amplification often takes on another agenda, which has no place in worship. Andy Crouch puts it this way:

Singing used to flourish in Protestant churches for a theological reason. Protestants believed and taught the priesthood of all believers. But today we are witnessing the rise of a new priesthood—the ones with the (literal) power. Armed with microphones and amps, gleaming in the multi-hued brilliance of spotlights, the amplified people do for us what we cannot do for ourselves: make music, offer prayers, approach the unapproachable.[22]

Robin Leaver's tough words are right on target. He states, "Where church music is performed in a way in which the voice of the total congregation is ignored . . . it has ceased to be church music."[23] I hope Johansson is exaggerating when he says that "the primary purpose of excessively loud music is to make the self so powerful that listeners are forced to accede to the musician's statement."[24] But if that is true, so is the final line of his statement: "Such music is manipulative, coercive, and mind deadening to say the least. Musical coercion in the church should be anathema."[25]

Amplification is too important a factor in worship to be ignored; pastors and worship planners must learn to use it sensitively. One place to begin is by giving attention to the ages of those manning the sound board on Sunday morning. The desire for greater volume tends to decrease with age. Technique and technology must never be allowed to become obvious in the service and must always be viewed as a means to a greater end—the glory of God.

## INSTRUMENTATION

Instrumentation has been a point of contention in many churches, and advocates of newer music have advanced their agenda under the motto "anything but organ." Robert Webber identifies one reason for this prejudice: "[People] assume that worship is primarily music and that worship renewal is linked with contemporary instrumentation."[26] Renewing worship is never as simple as buying a drum kit or electronic keyboard. Yet there's no avoiding the fact that Christian music has tended to mimic its cultural counterpart in style and instrumentation.

That raises the question of whether worship—and worship music in particular—should be viewed as a point of attraction for those outside the church. In his thoughtful book *Stones for Bread*, Daniel Frankforter contends that the argument which holds that "the church has always employed the culture's music to attract people" is misplaced nowadays because the cultural gap between church and world is so great. While Luther may have employed popular folk tunes for the people of the sixteenth century, says Frankforter, the distance between the church and the culture that produced those folk tunes was not nearly as great as the gulf that now exists between the church and society.[27] There is too great a distance between the music of the streets and the music of the church. This is true, and shows also why the current generation of worshipers will not easily accept classical hymnody and organ music—it's too culturally distant. No generation is likely to adopt a faith that cannot be interpreted through the musical language that it speaks.

Why did the organ become the dominant instrument in church music over the past several centuries? Robert Webber offers this explanation:

> The world view of the Middle Ages was strongly influenced by the Platonic concept of harmony. The harmony of the world and society was also a Christian conviction. Harmony was considered an expression of closeness to God. Music, particularly harmonious music, was viewed as an expression of God's harmony. The organ, it was observed, was the best instrument to express that harmony. The medieval church created a form of "Christian music" characterized by harmony.[28]

Things have changed. Modern hymn writer Brian Wren traces the shift: "Music has three main elements: melody, harmony, and rhythm.

In Western music, melody was dominant during the era of plainsong; later harmony came to prominence. In contemporary music, rhythm takes center stage."[29] It is no wonder, then, that modern musicians are choosing different instruments with which to accompany their songs. In the battle between the pipe organ and the drums, the drums have emerged as the victor. As one who enjoys the music of the pipe organ, I hope we can find creative ways to keep organs playing in our churches, for there is a priceless body of music that is best suited for that instrument. Yet instrumentation is adapting itself to the newer music, and that is a positive thing. Wren again—

> In worship music as elsewhere, different dialects need different instruments. For a melody, a solo violin or flute is excellent but can add little to harmony on its own, even when racing up and down in arpeggios. A well-played drum set gives good rhythms but does almost nothing for melody; the pipe organ is fine for melody and harmony but hard to play very rhythmically. Thus in contemporary worship instrumentation moves away from the organ on to the guitar (which can provide rhythm and harmony) and piano (which is pretty good for all three).[30]

Music is the common language of a congregation, and pastoral sensitivity and patience will be required when making changes to it. The best approach is to make the worship that employs newer music both spiritually deep and inviting. Just as younger Christians feel excluded in churches that use music from the seventeenth and eighteenth centuries, older believers feel disinvited when they are asked to worship with unfamiliar music. Music must be a means of including people in worship, not excluding them.

## DEFUSING CONFLICT

Music isn't neutral. It will be either an asset or a liability to the church and its worship. Which it will be depends on understanding the role music plays in worship, finding the right people to carry out that role, and keeping music subservient to the church's broader call to be a worshiping community. That's a dicey assignment.

Here are four areas of potential conflict concerning worship music, along with some ideas for how to defuse them.

## MUSIC SELECTION

Music selection can be a minefield for pastors, especially in churches having volunteer musicians. Yet the potential for either good or harm is so great that it's best for pastors to err on the side of overfunctioning. In practical terms, this means that when there is any question about the ability of staff members to adequately select music for worship, the pastor should do it him- or herself. While it should be a long-term goal to train others to function in this area, it's too important a task to be done poorly.

In selecting music for worship, textual content is the single most important factor to be considered. If a song's lyrics do not accurately communicate Christian truth appropriate for the occasion, it should not be used. Brian Wren says that "though the words we sing are only part of the experience of singing, they deserve critical attention because they either enlarge and develop Christian faith or distort and diminish it."[31]

Another significant consideration is singability. In practical terms, this means asking whether or not the congregation can sing the song. I recently attended a church that would be considered on the cutting edge in most ways. Given the attention this church gave to attracting and engaging seekers, it was surprising to see that most of its worship music was known only to the band; the congregation didn't sing at all. In an informal conversation after the service, three regular attendees made unsolicited comments about the frustration of being asked to learn new music week after week. That frustration can be avoided by careful planning.

## HYMNS

Hymns contain more biblical and theological content than many of the books in a pastor's library. What pastor wouldn't want phrases like "And can it be that I should gain an int'rest in the Savior's blood?" running through parishioners' minds throughout the week? Also, many hymns are prayers addressed to God. Augustine said that "he who sings, prays twice." The use of good hymn texts and reminding people that they are singing a prayer to God is a good way to enhance the corporate prayer life of the church.

But hymn singing can be a stretch for many worshipers these days. Hymns must be done well if they are to be received positively. These tips are useful for worship planners.[32]

- Be realistic. It's better to know ten or twelve hymns well, than thirty perfunctorily.

- Choose hymns first on the basis of text, then singability.

- Find alternate tunes for good hymn texts. Use the metrical index, found in any good hymnbook, to find more singable or better-known tunes for a hymn.

- Don't use terms like *formal, classic,* or *old* when introducing hymns because they may prejudice people against the hymn.

- Print good hymn texts in the bulletin or in church newsletters as a way of encouraging people to use them devotionally. (Be aware the permission from a copyright holder may be required.)

- Prepare, plan, and implement hymns carefully so that the congregation will not have a bad experience at singing hymns.

- Introduce new hymns subtly, yet consistently, over a period of several weeks. Build familiarity by using them as preludes, offertories, or choir anthems.

**APPLAUSE**

The use of applause in church can be a touchy subject, which is precisely the reason it needs to be considered carefully. Not long ago applause was seldom or never heard in churches. In our culture, applause is the accepted means of expressing approval or affirmation. So people wishing to make a positive gesture in a public setting most often applaud. While the practice seems irreverent to some, applauding in church is not an unforgivable breach of liturgical protocol. Having said that, I confess that, with some rare exceptions, I do not applaud in church. I have come to this personal position for three reasons.

First, musical offerings in church are made to God and not to me. Thus, who am I to presume to accept the choir's anthem or the vocalist's solo? While I occasionally offer a hearty "well done" to musicians after a service, I do not clap for them.

Second, applauding seems to me to be an insufficient response in worship. Clapping is too pedestrian. It is what everyone does everywhere—at the ballpark, at the symphony, at political rallies. In the worship of God, I want to use some other sign of pleasure, joy, or approval. This has been the purpose behind uttering words such as "Hallelujah," "Amen," and "Praise God" during worship. Perhaps we should teach people such higher ways of expressing themselves rather than merely adopting the common practice of our profane culture.

Third, I don't clap in church because I fear it too often gives the impression of elevating certain gifts beyond others. For example, applauding a soloist may be a way of affirming the musician's gift, but what message is sent when we do not applaud for other offerings? What about those who care for infants in the church nursery so that we may hear the solo? What about those who volunteer time to clean the church building or those who greet attendees at the door or offer prayers or testimonies during worship? Enlisting soloists is a lot easier—and less important to the church in the long run—than enlisting nursery workers. It seems counterproductive to affirm public gifts by applause while ignoring the service of those who work behind the scenes.

## RECORDED MUSIC

The student newspaper at the institution where I teach has the endearing habit of publishing classroom quotes from professors. One day I saw myself quoted as saying, "Evangelicals invented karaoke; we call it 'special music.'" The quote was accurate, if a bit hyperbolic. Increasingly, however, there is nothing special about the music offered to God in worship. During the opening service of a camp meeting a few years ago, the choir sang its first anthem of the camp. This group of volunteers hadn't sung together prior to their one and only rehearsal an hour before the service. The quality of sound produced by this makeshift choir belied its amateur status. I listened in amazement until it occurred to me that not only was the choir using a recorded accompaniment but their voices also were supplanted by a recording of a professional choir. People have lost Grammy awards for that kind of tacky imitation. Should we resort to lip synching our praise to God?

The use of recorded accompaniments swept through the church in the 1970s and 80s. Interestingly, the trend has abated in recent years, perhaps due to generational tastes. "Canned" music is perceived as less than authentic by the younger generation. Musically speaking, this is a positive development. Using technology to create a professional sounding solo performance is a double-edged sword. Church is family, and family isn't always nice, neat, and perfect. While worship, and particularly music, should always aim high, it should be an honest offering by the members of that congregation who are doing their best. Terri Bocklund McLean captures exactly the problem with using recorded tracks of instrumental accompaniments:

> Chiefly they lack the element of visible human craft; they lack a vital interaction between people and leader and they tell all that come through the doors that, "we don't have anyone here good enough to lead us and haven't made it a priority to find anyone good enough to lead us, so we've put our leadership in a can." The saddest result of using "canned music" is the

inevitable impoverishment of the community. It is far better to use the human gifts of the congregation, even when they are humble, and to pray and speak the needs, waiting on God to raise the leaders and the talent to match the vision.[33]

Music is, as Thomas Long puts it, a nuclear reactor in the church. It is a reservoir of potential energy for good—but it can also melt down and cause great harm. That need not occur. The secret to using this kind of energy is vigilance on the part of pastors and musicians. Constant attentiveness and refusing to ever forget that music is a central feature in the worship life of the church can enable a congregation to harness this virtually infinite source of energy to the glory of God and to the edification of the body of Christ.

## CHAPTER NINE

# STYLES

## *Putting Preference in Perspective*

—⟋⟍⟍⟋—

*It is the voice of the church that is heard in singing together. It is not you who sings, it is the church that is singing, and you as a member of the church may share in its song.*
—Dietrich Bonhoeffer

> ### SILVER BULLET
> Unity results when music ministry is focused on serving the congregation.

It is surely an irony that delights the Enemy and grieves the Holy Spirit—Christians fighting with each other over worship. The incongruity of this leaves me vacillating between anger and embarrassment. For better or worse, much of the actual combat takes place in the arena of music. It need not be so—in fact, it *must* not be so. Pastors can help to right this situation by enabling their congregations to see the utter silliness of such battles. They are both counterproductive within the church and subject her to ridicule by the unbelieving world.

Ultimately, what should keep us from engaging in congregational warfare over music is our doctrine of the church. When people fully understand what the church is called to be, fighting about music will seem ridiculous even for those who are most adamant about their preferred musical style. There is no other way to resolve this conflict. No measure of liturgical innovation will suffice to cover ecclesiological failure. Worship is a lightning rod, a place where other problems gather. Trying to smooth over the musical turmoil within a congregation that has no sound ecclesiology is an exercise in futility. But with a solid commitment to take the call of the church seriously, it is possible for the church to sing a new song, and to sing it in the key of love. There are ways to do this without choosing sides musically. I suggest three.

## COMMIT TO MUSICAL EXCELLENCE

A first step toward building unity in the church's worship music is to pursue musical excellence. To speak realistically about musical excellence, it is necessary speak of it in the context of a particular congregation, because the standard for what constitutes excellence will vary from church to church. The college church I served for several years enjoyed the advantages of having a school of music on campus and an unusually large number of members having some form of musical training. Musical excellence for that congregation was measured by a different standard from the smaller churches I have served, which lacked those resources. So to encourage musical excellence is not to call for all churches to sound the same. It is to ask churches to make a commitment to do the very best they can musically for the glory of God.

### FUNCTIONAL EXCELLENCE

Thomas Long reminds us that church music serves the needs of the people so that any talk of excellence in music must begin with the congregation in focus.

> The first mark of musical excellence in worship is a functional one. Good music is that which empowers the congregation and gives the congregation a means to express the thoughts and feelings of their worship. If a hymn or other musical piece is beyond a congregation's range or reach it

cannot be called excellent, no matter how superb it may be on internal and technical grounds.[1]

To attempt music that is beyond the reach of the congregation does not produce musical excellence. Church music is not created in a vacuum; it is created within the context of corporate worship and edification. And nothing is to be gained by ceding control of the church's music program to a few professionals under the guise of achieving excellence. The entire congregation must be involved in making music.

## THEOLOGICAL EXCELLENCE

In the pursuit of musical excellence, theology must trump all other concerns. Terri Bocklund McLean, who champions the use of new music in the church, insists that "good worship music should be God-centered and people-related."[2] She adds that "theology prevents music from assuming an independent role in the worship of the church."[3]

A student of mine who served a part-time pastoral charge dealt with a church organist who was an accomplished musician and who insisted on playing classical pieces that had no theological relevance for the church or its worship. Because the music was well done, the organist thought she was serving the end of musical excellence. Yet the student pastor noticed that the congregation's attention wandered during these musical offerings. He correctly concluded that the organist's contribution, however competent, was misguided.

Church musicians must begin their task by asking theological questions. Is the text theologically sound? Does the style contribute to or disrupt worship? Does the piece engage the congregation in the liturgy? Again, these questions must be contextualized for each congregation. There will always be musical diversity among churches, so the question is not "How well is the music performed?" or "Do the people like it?" but "Is the music theologically appropriate for *this*

147

context?" Brian Wren suggests that music in the church should always aim to be one or more of the following:[4]

- *Formative,* shaping and modeling our faith as it tells a story within the whole story of God in Christ and draws us into the drama of God's saving love
- *Transformative,* moving us from isolation to belonging, indifference to interest, interest to conviction, and conviction to commitment
- *Cognitive,* giving us something to think about
- *Educational,* teaching us something we didn't know about the Bible, the church, or Christian faith
- *Inspirational,* lifting us out of ourselves into hope, joy, and peace

## LITURGICAL EXCELLENCE

Music also works best when it is a good fit liturgically, that is when it is used at the right point in a service. Bocklund McLean is helpful at this point.

Certain songs are particularly useful for certain elements of worship. A praise song generally can't do the job of a sending song, and a song sung from the perspective of the individual can't do the job of a gathering song. What we need is a common-sense approach to using songs in a way that helps make the worship experience seamless and flowing. Such an approach requires that the choice of music serve the ultimate goal of successfully engaging the community in worship.[5]

In some services that do not flow well, the problem isn't so much *what* is sung as *when* it is sung. Nothing interrupts liturgical progression quite as abruptly as a song that heads in a different direction from the rest of the liturgy. In this regard, pastors and worship leaders need to be sensitive in the ways they respond publicly to musical offerings. How unseemly is it to follow a musical offering that has been obviously moving to the congregation by launching into an announcement about the next church work day. Part of achieving musical excellence is allowing music to have its full effect. Sometimes that means being quiet long enough to allow the Spirit to finish what He's doing through the music. At other times, a well-placed "amen" from the pastor may be invaluable.

## STRATEGIC EXCELLENCE

Musical excellence involves exercising care when music is selected, but it also requires regular review of the church's music to ensure that it is accomplishing the ends for which it was chosen. To make a commitment to pursue excellence in the church's music ministry is to make a pledge to train the congregation. Good music ministries are conducted not by good musicians alone but also by good congregations. Ascertaining where the people are musically, where they should be, and how to get them there is the only agenda most churches need to conduct a worship retreat.

Dieting involves more than looking at pictures of exercise equipment, and making improvements in a church's worship music involves more than just listening to CDs. It requires helping the congregation learn new music so they can sing it with gusto. A congregation in Pittsburgh produces a CD of new worship music each year for the purpose of teaching music to the congregation. By listening to the CD, people are able to learn the music without taking time out of the worship service.[6] There are many other ways to teach music. By whatever means it happens, achieving musical excellence will not be accidental. It will come as the result of a commitment of leadership, resources, and manpower toward the worthy goal of gaining unity and clarity in the church's worship life.

## BE INTENTIONALLY ECLECTIC

A second step toward creating unity in the church's worship music is to be intentionally eclectic. Most churches become predictable in their music selection. Some stay with traditional hymnody and instrumentation; others opt for new music, typically involving some version of a worship band. A few churches try to do a bit of both. Given the culture we are attempting to reach and the increasingly global dimension of the church, pastors would do best to guide their churches toward musical eclecticism. By *eclecticism*, I mean openness to a wide variety of musical styles and to the worship practices of Christians from many cultures. This is necessary where the doctrine of the church is embraced in a healthy fashion by its members.

As every pastor and worship leader knows, not everyone likes every form of music. Yet the issue at stake is not personal preference but theological integrity. As a pastor, I must be willing to utilize musical forms I do not personally enjoy if they help the congregation to grow. Long notes that "an ethic of tolerance and mutual participation is required. People need to be willing to sing music they don't necessarily like for the sake of the unity of the body."[7] A church's ability to do this depends on the maturity of the congregation. So the move to musical eclecticism cannot be made unilaterally; it will be the result of a congregation's intentional embrace of its ecclesial calling in these times.

### THE OLD AND THE NEW

An immediate consequence of adopting an eclectic approach to music ministry is that a church will have to be prepared to both embrace new worship music and continue to employ the best of the "old" music that has earned its place in the church. It is difficult to see why this has been such a challenging adjustment for many churches, because there has always been diversity within the worship life of the church. A quick scan through the psalms, for example, reveals an incredible range of music. There are elaborately written acrostic poems, joyful songs with refrains, personal expressions of inner faith, and angst-filled calls for revenge. Eclecticism in church music is a return to our liturgical heritage, not a deviation from it.

Nevertheless, some churches struggle to include more than one style of music in their repertoire. For a long time, some congregations resisted adopting newer music because some of it originated in Pentecostal or charismatic gatherings. Happily, this bias is disappearing. The worship renewal movement has strengthened worship, particularly in the area of personal engagement in music. To open ourselves to the best of other Christian traditions can only deepen the worship of our congregations when we do so carefully and thoughtfully.

In like fashion, the move to eclecticism commits the church to nourishing its vital link to its musical past. While embracing the newer music used in worship, we must continue to treasure, for example, Bernard of Clairvaux's thirteenth-century hymn, "Jesus, the Very Thought of Thee." To be musically linked with brothers and sisters in the faith from centuries past is one meaning of the "communion of the saints." Of course, maintaining this link will mean finding new and creative ways to utilize such music. Simply imposing medieval or Renaissance music on modern congregations isn't likely to be effective. But by using alternate tunes, adjusting tempos, or creating new arrangements, we can help modern believers rejoice in the treasury of our musical heritage. As Robb Redman put it, "To sing a familiar hymn with a new arrangement is like meeting an old friend in new clothes."[8]

Every congregation is different, of course, but it's hard to imagine any congregation that doesn't have a limit for the amount of change they can absorb and the rate at which they can absorb it. Many church musicians overestimate a congregation's ability to learn new music. Realistically, if a church learns a dozen or so new pieces over the course of a year, it has done well. It's far preferable to proceed slowly and have people thinking that they should speed up rather than to create frustration among worshipers who then sit passively as the well-intentioned worship team tries to teach yet one more new song. Brian Wren suggests several strategies for teaching songs and repeating them so they become part of the congregation's repertoire. The following are his suggestions with my commentary.[9]

1. *Find and use people's favorite hymns and songs.* If we respect what people know and use it appropriately, they are more likely to trust us when we offer something new.

2. *Think in terms of generations but not stereotypes.* In the little country church I attend, we were inundated each Sunday with college students. When surveyed, they revealed one reason they chose to attend our church: "Because you sing hymns." Don't presume to know people's musical tastes without asking.

3. *Respect the contract of enjoyment.* In practical terms, this means that if you choose three songs people know, they will accept the choice of one song they don't.

4. *Look over the lectionary wall.* Churches that use the lectionary can sometimes becomes slaves to it, especially in the selection of music. One or two lectionary-minded songs each week are enough.

5. *When introducing a new song, begin with the words.* Ask, "Are these words worth singing? Do we believe what they say?" Allow people to dwell on their meaning as spoken and to experience their power. Make sure people believe the text is worthy of their attention.

6. *Unless the tune is instantly accessible, allow the congregation to hear it several times before singing it.* The suggestions made in the previous chapter in regard to hymn singing apply here also.

7. *Teach new songs in happy social situations.* There's a right time and a wrong time to introduce new music. Right after the pastor has announced his or her resignation is probably not the right time.

8. *Repeat a new song two or three times within the first six months after it's introduced.* Good teachers know that learning has to be reinforced. That is all the more true of church music. Use it or lose it.

9. *Sing brief congregational songs on every possible occasion.*

Potluck suppers and prayer meetings are ideal occasions for singing. The Christian church is one of the few places in our culture where people still sing together. Affirm that whenever possible. Singing binds people together.

10. *Connect the song repertoires of Sunday school, vacation Bible school, summer camp, and the worshiping congregation.* This requires a big-picture approach to music ministry, but it will pay big dividends. At a minimum, it could prevent every subsystem within the church from having a private worship culture.

11. *Don't teach anything that must be denied in order to grow.* Stay away from texts and music that may be theologically questionable or considered offensive. There are lyrics, both old and new, that are not helpful in the messages they convey. Be disciplined enough to say no to such music.

12. *Keep record of what is sung.* As a young pastor in a large, college-dominated congregation, I found myself more intimidated by having to select music than by preparing and preaching sermons. Happily, this church had kept copies of all Sunday bulletins and had them bound each year. This was a priceless resource during my early tenure there. I could familiarize myself with the congregation's worship history and determine which songs were familiar to them and which were new. A musical record is a wonderful gift to give to the future of your church.

## BLENDED WORSHIP

Blended worship, as defined by Robert Webber,

> draws from the biblical and historical sources that have faced the changes in traditional worship, but it is equally a concern to draw from contemporary worship. For this reason, blended worship is characterized by these three concerns: (1) to be rooted in the biblical and early church tradition; (2) to draw from the resources of the entire church; (3) a radical commitment to contemporary relevance.[10]

This approach is ideal in the sense that it clearly evinces a healthy and outward focused eclecticism. Yet it may be more than ideal; it may be idealistic. Blending worship is easier said than done. Many attempts wind up resembling the buffet table at Ponderosa: There are a lot of items there, but they don't seem to go together. To do blended worship consistently and well depends on having a mature and forward-looking congregation. It would be a stretch for a congregation having recently fought a worship war to jump right in to blended worship. Realistically, most congregations need to move incrementally in this direction, with great wisdom and patience on the part of the pastoral leaders.

## ALTERNATIVE WORSHIP

Yet another approach to eclecticism is seen in the alternative approach to worship seen in the emergent church worship, what Webber calls the Ancient-Future Faith. This approach cultivates the church's historical ties to older liturgical practice, reinventing them in creative ways to be more fluent with today's culture. This edgier approach to worship is perhaps best suited to newer congregations, particularly in cities, than for established suburban congregations. Yet we remember that the Holy Spirit is like the wind: He blows where He wills.

Musical eclecticism is a wonderful way to help believers grasp the communal aspect of the church and come to understand that the church has a primary purpose other than meeting their needs. It invites them to become part of something bigger than themselves, to lose themselves in order to find themselves. This will be a distinguishing characteristic of vital churches in the days ahead. According to Leonard Sweet, who has provided provocative looks at church and culture, musical eclecticism is a correction to the praise revolution. Sweet observes that postmodern Christians need to be "bi-musical," that is, they must be able to express their belief in more than one musical tradition and know a second musical language almost as well as their own.[11] The miracle of the church on Pentecost was that everyone heard the good news in his or her own language. Could it be that through embracing other musical dialects, the modern church could liturgically incarnate that Pentecostal reality once again?

## FOCUS CONGREGATIONALLY

The third critical element in leading churches to sing together in unity is to insist that the focus of the entire music ministry be preeminently congregational. As a solution to the worship wars over music, this point can hardly be overemphasized.

### TRAINING MUSICIANS

Training the musicians is the place to begin when shifting the focus of a church's music ministry. It should be remembered that there is no necessary correlation between spiritual gifts and spiritual maturity. The mere possession of a gift or talent does not qualify one to use it in the church. Too often, gifted but immature musicians are turned loose to "minister" to a congregation. Their lack of maturity in the faith immediately sets the music ministry off track. Terri Bocklund McLean writes that "what is required to encourage relevant and authentic music worship among the congregation is a band [or leader] that knows it is not the 'star' of the worship gathering. The band must operate on the understanding that the time of worship is about God, not the band."[12] Church musicians who are self-focused may produce a good show, but no church will grow under their leadership. Churches would do well to work out in advance, and have in writing, the expectations that will be placed on those who participate in the music ministry of the church. Those expectations should be mission driven, clearly articulated, and unapologetically executed.

Long is right when he says that "the emphasis in music should always be on congregational music, rather than the offerings of highly skilled musicians."[13] That's one reason the zenith of so-called special music has passed. Liturgically speaking, performance music, with some exceptions, does not accomplish what congregational participation does. While there may be some danger that we will neglect the musical gifts some people have been given for edifying the body, there is much to be gained by decreasing the use of performance music in worship. There will always be other creative ways to employ gifted musicians that do not come at the expense of "the work of the people."

To keep the church's music ministry focused on the congregation, it's necessary to have mechanisms for gaining feedback about music from the congregation in a manner that does not cause musicians to become defensive.

## UNDERSTANDING MUSIC

Having a clear understanding of the nature of congregational music will enable pastors and musicians to operate on the basis of sound principles rather than at the mercy of something as fickle as culture. In his excellent book *Praying Twice: The Music and Words of Congregational Song*, Brian Wren argues that congregational song should adhere to seven basic indicatives.[14]

1. *It is corporate.* Congregational song should be corporate, because singing together brings us together. Congregations singing together are agreeing not to be soloists but to join their voices, to keep the same tempo, to, in effect, love each other in the act of singing. The corporate nature of the song is signaled by the fact that no individual voice is heard, no single participant receives recognition.

2. *It is corporeal.* Congregational singing is corporeal in that it is a body experience. It stimulates heightened awareness, alertness, and excitement. The movement through dance and bodily involvement seen in much modern worship is something of a return to a pattern often seen in Scripture.

3. *It is inclusive.* Congregational singing includes everyone. Almost anyone can sing, and everyone can make a joyful noise. Inclusivity in

song is a theological value, the corollary of unity. The congregation cannot demonstrate its unity in Christ if people are shut out from its song. It is vitally important that *everyone* be invited into the church's song, not just the elite.

4. *It is credal.* Congregational singing helps us express a believing response in a self-committing way. When a tune is consistently sung with a particular text, it gains power over our memories. The creedal power of congregational song has pastoral implications because people made speechless or speech impaired through illness or injury are often still able to sing.

5. *It is ecclesial.* In the act of singing, the members not only support one another but proclaim the community of faith reaching beyond the congregation that sings. Thus, the corporate inclusiveness of congregational song is ecclesial: It declares what the church aims and hopes to be and reminds the singers of their common faith and hope.

6. *It is inspirational.* Congregational singing is inspirational in that it lifts us out of the mundane and the ordinary.

7. *It is evangelical.* Unbelievers come to church not primarily to investigate the claims of Christ but to investigate the Christ in us. When congregational song is in good health, it demonstrates love relationships of the children of God perhaps better than any other thing we do in public worship.

These seven principles are a poignant reminder of why the church has found music to be perhaps the single most powerful device for engaging the community of faith in worship that is God-honoring, edifying, and bears eloquent witness to the faith. To build a music ministry that aims at such an understanding of congregational singing is to proactively address the underlying symptoms of the worship wars.

Many who read these words will not be trained musicians and may feel out of their element in asserting leadership over the church's music ministry. But nothing can replace pastoral leadership in the worship life of the church. That leadership need not be heavy-handed or, indeed, any particular style at all. What is needed to bring unity to a church's music ministry is the ongoing interest and involvement of a caring shepherd. And that doesn't require the ability to read music! When we treat people with respect and choose music with the primary aim of enabling people to worship God, good things will happen.

Brian Wren, upon whose work so much of this chapter rests, issues the reminder that when directing the music ministry of the church, it is important to "let God be God."[15] Many pastors, I include myself, are either control freaks or people pleasers—or both. We must constantly remind ourselves that the church belongs to God. His desire is that His body will reflect His glory, will dwell in the shalom of His presence, and will worship Him in spirit and in truth. As we trust God whole-heartedly and take thoughtful steps in leading His people, this vision of the church is not an impossible dream. It is our destiny.

## CHAPTER TEN

# AESTHETICS

## Returning Worship to Its Senses

—⟨⟨⟨—

*Instrumental music, visual art, and the architectural*
*space create expectations for worship before*
*any words are spoken.*
—Tex Sample

### SILVER BULLET
People worship fully when their senses are fully engaged.

The only Catholic church I attended as a child was a historic mission on a Native-American reservation near Tucson, Arizona, my hometown. I can still recall the feeling I had upon entering that church. It was as if I'd suddenly entered an alien world. The small Protestant church my family attended was sparsely decorated. It had uniformly low ceilings, a chancel that centered around a pulpit, an altar railing, and absolutely nothing on the walls save for one copy of a popular painting of Jesus. This old mission church, in continual use from its founding in the seventeenth century, presented a veritable assault on the senses. The ceilings were high with frescoes painted everywhere. There were statues of various saints and angelic figures tucked into every corner and cranny of the place. While there was a small pulpit that appeared to be serviceable for preaching, the front of this church was wholly taken up with an altar. Unlike the spindly railing at the front of my church, this altar was an ornate table that appeared to have been made by a group of artisans working by the hour. It was huge, colorful, and impressive. The old mission touched even my sense of smell as incense and aromatic candles burned at various places in the church.

The difference between these two houses of worship could not have been more stark. As a boy, I was unsure how to process what I had seen. For years I was satisfied with the explanation offered by conservative Protestantism that Catholics were "into idols." But as I grew both in my own faith and in my understanding of Roman Catholic theology, I saw the inadequacy of such explanations. As a theology student, I learned of other worship traditions within Protestantism, and I discovered that not every church adopted as austere an attitude toward the use of visual elements in worship as did the church of my youth. I found that many churches made use of sculpture, paintings, and even architecture itself in their worship.

I am more than content to locate myself within the Protestant tradition, yet I am convinced that the wholesale removal of the arts from worship was a mistake made by many Protestants—a mistake which, happily, is now being corrected. The senses are used to absorb powerful nonverbal messages. That makes the arts extremely important for worship and for worship planners.

## THE VALUE OF ART IN WORSHIP

Trying to separate art from worship is like trying to divorce sexuality from marriage. It is possible to have a sexless marriage, but not a truly fulfilling one, or not for long. Theologians have held for centuries that the artistic impulse, the desire to create works of beauty and imagination, is a part of our God-given impulse to worship. Thus, to separate art and worship is to violate the intent of the Creator himself. Thomas Long says that "there is a profound sense in which authentic Christian worship is theater." Long cites Robert Webber's contention that "Christian worship is drama, in the sense that it is both a dramatic retelling and a dramatic re-enactment of the biblical story," and continues, "Therefore congregations don't make worship dramatic, instead they should be concerned about how to allow the drama already present at worship to be brought to the surface, to be more deeply experienced."[1] Christian worship is artistic through and through. To plan a weekly liturgy can be every bit as artistically expressive as to create a painting or sculpture. Even pastors who have difficulty drawing stick figures can express their artistic inclination by constructing a worship experience and preparing and preaching sermons. If this be the case, then art in general ought to find a warm welcome in the church.

The fact that art has had difficulty finding acceptance, particularly within conservative Protestantism, says something about both the church's failure to heed its own doctrine of Creation and the propensity of human beings to turn for evil purposes the good gifts of the Creator. Recovering our understanding of Creation and finding ways to channel creative gifts into activities that honor the Creator have as much to do with worship renewal as does selecting proper music or constructing viable liturgies. In an informative book titled *Enter His Courts with Praise: A Study of the Role of Music and the Arts in Worship*, Robert Webber notes that in the Old Testament, "art communicated truth about God. Art communicated the beauty, the sovereignty, the holiness of God. Worshipers met the God of beauty and holiness through the truth spoken by the art and symbolism of the temple."[2] The close relationship between art and worship contradicts the austerity of much of the Christian tradition. The Reformers' reaction to the arts was mostly an overreaction to Catholicism's propensity for using art to teach and defend some of the doctrines the Reformers had rejected, including the veneration of saints, the cult of Mary, and the elevation of tradition. Certainly, many Protestant leaders saw the danger of idolatry in connection with the arts, but as James White notes, this was a response that reached further than was warranted.

Those who destroyed liturgical art in the past recognized clearly its religious power. But they feared that ignorant people might confuse the mirror with what is reflected. This is probably the least dangerous form of idolatry we face today. Indeed, when liturgical art calls us from indulging in egocentric satisfying of our own emotions and self-centered lives, it can break down a far worse form of idolatry.[3]

This dynamic is now being played out in Protestant churches. Pastors and worship leaders are recognizing the value of art in prompting people to look beyond the self—the real source of idolatry—and to consider the timeless issues of truth, beauty, and the human predicament that are so easily evoked by art.

## USING ART IN WORSHIP

To give art and aesthetics their proper place in worship is not to adopt a New Age approach to worship, as some may fear. The revelation of God is bigger than any of us can imagine, and it will break through into our lives in numberless ways. Not the least of those ways are expressions of beauty and creativity by human beings. The fact that Jesus lived and worked—as an artisan, no less—among us lends dignity to the human creative and artistic impulse and gives value to that which is physical and material. The arts, perhaps better than any other vehicle, afford human beings the ability to express all aspects of life as created beings. Surely we will want those expressions that reveal the pathos and depths of human emotion to be present in worship.

### UNLEASHING IMAGINATION

To use art properly in worship involves more than forming a banner committee or buying a painting for the foyer. The liturgical use of art requires tapping the spontaneity of a congregation's giftedness and channeling that creativity in ways that help to reveal God. One formidable hurdle to be cleared in so doing is the culture of instant gratification that affects worship in so many ways. We are working with people who have been visually bombarded throughout every waking moment of the week. Moreover, the images that have been employed to sell, influence, and persuade are usually not subtle; they leave little or nothing to the imagination. But good art is imaginative beyond all else. William B. Hendricks highlights this cultural dilemma:

It is been said, that in ancient Greece, art killed religion; later in Christian Europe religion killed art. That alone is worth some reflection. But we can add that in modern America, entertainment is killing both art and religion—the situation that leaves very little space for the Christian artist.[4]

What makes art so conversant with spirituality is its demand for contemplation and submission. Consumers are not known for their patience, so the use of art in the church faces some uphill cultural battles. Yet some churches are finding innovative ways to employ art, like sponsoring shows featuring the work of church members, hiring staff people devoted to cultivating artistic expression in the church, and, yes, forming banner committees. I suspect that Robb Redman is right when he says, regarding art in the church, "The crisis that faces most churches is not a lack of resources but rather the failure of imagination to use the resources God has already given."[5] God brings into nearly every local church an amazing array of gifts and talents. To unleash the gifts of the people of God, including artistic gifts, is a key to becoming a healthy, mission-driven church.

## USING ART WELL

The practical use of art in worship requires careful thought. Robert Webber offers three helpful guidelines.[6]

First, "art should be characterized by simplicity; it should not be smothered by explanation and an abundance of words, which destroy the mystery; nor should it be so complex that the message remains hidden and obscure." Good art speaks for itself, and pastors should refrain from trying to explain a work of art.

Second, "art should be well executed. When music, drama, dance, or environmental symbols such as banners, are shoddy, they reflect poorly upon the message they represent. When characterized by excellence, they express the beauty, the majesty and mystery of God." Just as pastors would not allow someone who can't carry a tune to sing a solo in church, we ought to prevent bad art from becoming a distraction from worship.

Third, Webber suggests that "art should be integrated with the flow of worship. Art in worship is not a performance directed toward the people, rather art supports the acts of gathering, hearing the word, giving thanks, and sending forth." The guidelines for making music liturgically appropriate apply to art as well. There is a world of difference when, for example, liturgical dance is conducted within the rhythm and flow of the liturgy rather than being used simply as an avant-garde expression of worship. Context is everything.

## EXPLORING POSSIBILITIES

I have friends in ministry in Australia who have centered their outreach for Christ in the arts. They understand that the lifeblood of a culture, what it truly believes and says about itself, is seen first and foremost in its music, films, and visual arts. Churches that find ways to connect the basic human need to interpret life through art to their liturgy will have an inroad into the culture that cannot be attained in any other way. We are visual, not just aural, creatures. We see as well as hear. For too long Protestant worship has been focused on reaching people through the ear alone. Finding ways to visually express the grandeur and majesty of God, the glory of His Creation, and the grace that surrounds human life will enhance the ability of our people to "enter his courts with praise."

There is room in worship for the dramatic and rhetorical arts as well. Many churches use drama, to varying effect, and there is a growing library of material available for this purpose. Pastors might also consider establishing a lay readers group, whose purpose would be to communicate Scripture clearly and effectively. If the lectionary is used or if the pastor plans sermon texts well in advance, a lay readers group will have adequate time to find creative ways to share the Word of God with the congregation, including dramatic re-creations, antiphonal readings, or simple choral readings.

## EXPLORING SACRED SPACE

While the church of my youth was plain and artistically desolate, it was nevertheless a special place to me. It seemed so largely because of the teachings of my father, who managed to put "the fear of God" into me concerning respect for that sacred space. Running in the church building or being excessively loud, even after the service, was considered a breach of propriety, the punishment for which I dared not imagine. As a child of Charlie Walters, one learned early not to "carry on" in God's house. My father's attitude toward the church building seems a bit austere now, yet it was from him—a conservative Protestant to the core, a man who would have been appalled to see a piece of artwork prominently displayed in a sanctuary—that I gained a sense of sacred space.

### THE REALITY OF SACRED SPACE

There is, it seems, such a thing as "holy ground." Most of us find special places in our lives where God seems closer somehow, easier to hear. It may simply be that in those places we pay closer attention to God, but still, we commune with Him more intensely and with more openness in those locales. It is true that we believers are "the temple of the Holy Spirit" and that God does not dwell in "temples made of hands." We accept the reality of the indwelling of God's Spirit in His church, which is a people, not a building. Yet there is something unique about sacred space. In spite of the fact that my own view of ecclesiology is evolving toward one that eschews the owning of property, I realize that whenever

I walk into a cathedral, there emerges a perspective of God that I almost never encounter elsewhere.

It is significant that the book of Exodus, the foundational story of Israel's deliverance and formation as God's covenant people, is largely devoted to detailed instructions for the construction of a tent. There's something theologically profound about that. Having a place dedicated to the worship of God by His people has been part of the Judeo-Christian tradition since the time of the Exodus. I'll admit that I sometimes imagine Moses placing the plans for the Tabernacle before the Israelites only to have someone holler, "Where's the basketball court?"

While there may be some arguments based on a desire for stewardship, outreach, and fellowship that favor the construction of "sancti-nasiums," there is perhaps a greater argument to be made for the construction of a space dedicated wholly to the worship of God. What would be the effect on the life of a church if its leaders were to say, "We can defer the construction of a gym for a year or two. For now, the worship of God must take precedence"? It would be exciting to be the pastor of such a group.

## THE NEED FOR SACRED SPACE

I learned the power of sacred space early in my pastorate at a college-based church. Because of the limited size of our church sanctuary, we held Sunday services in the larger college chapel, which was in most ways a suitable location. But college students attended chapel there several times a week. They also attended concerts and watched movies there. For those nineteen-year-old students, making the switch from viewing the building as a Saturday night theater to a Sunday morning temple of God was a bit of a stretch. It wasn't much easier for adults. When we began offering one of our multiple services in the church sanctuary, there was a noticeable response from students. Most people accede in some way to the concept of sacred space. That's one reason pastors need to take it seriously when planning worship.

That point was driven home to me by a visit to, of all places, the Alamo. Having lived in San Antonio early in our marriage, my wife and I returned to celebrate a wedding anniversary. A trip to the Alamo was obligatory. When we entered that sacred shrine of Texas history, I was reminded how people behave in sacred space—or at least how they are expected to behave. There were Texas Rangers on duty inside the Alamo, and I heard them, time and again, asking men to remove their hats. I've been told that one can be arrested for spitting inside the Alamo. The battle that took place at the Alamo happened more than 170 years ago, but that event is remembered as people pay their respects and visit the grounds. People enter the building with a sense of reverence.

For all of the accessibility created by the informality of modern worship, we have lost something worthwhile by the easy dismissal of sacred space. Daniel Frankforter states that "consecration is the product of an ongoing process of prayerful use. This means that it may take a lot of time to build a sacred space but a very little time to destroy one. All it takes to profane a sacred place is for people to begin to behave in it as they do elsewhere."[7] Pondering Frankforter's comment in the context of modern worship, one is forced to ask, "What do the Texas Rangers know that Christians have forgotten?"

## THE IMPORTANCE OF ARCHITECTURE

James White says that "church architecture not only reflects the way Christians worship, but architecture also shapes worship, or not uncommonly, misshapes it."[8] The most obvious example of this point is the number of church sanctuaries, most built more than forty years ago, that are making the transition to newer forms of worship difficult or impossible. The seating, chancel space, ceiling height, and acoustics were all designed for worship in a certain form. Even churches built much more recently, employing theater-style seating and spacious chancels, are beginning to show their age as alternative approaches to worship are being used, which eschews the toward-the-stage orientation. Architecture matters. It will, for good or ill, shape what congregations can do liturgically.

Some congregations must simply make do with what they have. Yet even when the church's architecture inhibits liturgical innovation, some minor alterations such as improved lighting, new seating arrangements, or different décor can make a noticeable difference. For congregations having the opportunity to construct dedicated worship space, it should be remembered that "a congregation's vision and conviction about worship are embodied in its buildings."[9]

## USES OF SACRED SPACE

As James White points out, "Christian worship is action that requires space. And it is a balancing act between paying attention to divine activity, divine presence, and arrangements to accommodate those who worship."[10] A grand, downtown cathedral is a wonderful place to sit and meditate, gaining a sense of God's presence. But you can forget trying to hear much of anything said there—the acoustics are terrible. It is no coincidence that congregational singing gained its real place in liturgy in small English meetinghouses, where the sound didn't have to travel through much open space. It is the rare pastor who has not longed for both a grand sanctuary and an intimate chapel in the same church. Since that is not likely to be the liturgical lot of most clergy, we must think carefully about how we use the spaces we do have. James White points to types of liturgical space that are commonly needed for Christian worship:

1. *Gathering space.* Usually referred to as the narthex or foyer, gathering space is often shortchanged in churches, especially older ones. A good rule of thumb is to allow gathering space of 30 to 50 percent of the seating space in the sanctuary. Having room for people to congregate and mill around is more important than many church building committees—who are generally concerned more about cost than about liturgy—may believe.

2. *Movement space.* Room for people to move around during worship is as important as seating capacity—perhaps more so. The width and number of aisles, crossways, and the space between seating rows will affect what the people can do in worship.

3. *Congregational space.* Congregational space is where people actually come together, and it should create a sense of intimacy if possible. Remember this principle: The bigger the building, the bigger the performance. A crowd of one hundred in a building intended for five hundred will likely feel like spectators watching a performance. It is more difficult to be passive in a building that is filled to capacity or nearly so. That is why it is often preferable to remain overcrowded in a smaller facility than to add another service that might be sparsely attended.

4. *Choir space.* Choir space is any space used for the choir or others involved in leading worship, including instrumentalists. The location and size of this space will be determined by the role assigned to these people in worship.

5. *Altar-Table space.* In churches whose liturgy is centered on the Eucharist, this is the most conspicuous space in the building. Though rarer in evangelical churches, altar space is sometimes included in building plans. If so, it should be utilized and not ignored or co-opted for other purposes.

6. *Baptismal space.* Baptism is intended to be a public ritual; therefore, baptismal space ought never to be tucked away in some obscure corner of the building. The community should be able to participate in this sacrament. Given that different modes of baptism are available, the space allotted for baptism need not be as expensive to construct as a built-in baptistery. Elegant baptismal fonts can be visible, accessible, and affordable, for churches whose polity allows their use.[11]

## THE PULPIT

The pulpit has fallen on hard times in modern worship, having been replaced, in some cases, by plastic lecterns or removed altogether.

Yet the pulpit is more than a piece of furniture. Its presence communicates the fact that it is the Word of God, not the communicator, that is most significant in preaching. While modern communicators often prefer to have no barrier between themselves and their audience, the absence of a pulpit tends to place too much attention on the messenger. The pulpit need not dominate the chancel, and there is no rule requiring the preacher to stand behind it. But the pulpit as a symbol of the Word continues to have value, and pastors would do well to let their congregations know why they use "the sacred desk."

## ACOUSTICS

Acoustics is a key consideration in designing worship because sound is more important than ever in the worship of the church. When people are unable to hear what is being offered in worship, they are unable to enter into it. That makes worship a spiritual and not just a musical issue.[12] Many churches try to save money by purchasing a less expensive sound system only to discover that it does not meet their need. Because every acoustical environment is different, it makes sense to employ the services of a reputable acoustical engineer before investing in sound equipment. When constructing worship space, remember that both spoken voice and music must be heard—not one or the other.

## DÉCOR

When making decisions about worship space, remember that "good worship space is not merely the result of decor; it is also the product of mature theological reflection about the nature of worship. Form follows function and well-planned sanctuaries communicate by their very design the kind of worship that takes place within."[13]

Being artistically and aesthetically sensitive does not come easily to some pastors. Yet one of the amazing things about the body of Christ is that God gives different gifts to different members. There is almost always someone in a local church who has good artistic and aesthetic instincts. And often, they've been hoping for an opportunity to use this ability for God and the church. Use them!

## BEAUTY OVER BEAST

Much more is at stake with the issue of including the arts in worship than the mere appreciation of beauty. The church's capacity to embrace the arts is a key to its gaining a hearing in postmodern culture. Geoffrey Wainwright expresses the critical nature of this opportunity:

> If the arts, as products of human culture, are relegated by Christianity to the secular sphere, they may assert themselves as a rival religion. The sociologist, R. Bocock considers that the development of secular art and entertainment in the west "has probably been much more significant in affecting church attendance than the growth of science as an alternative belief system." Bocock blames historical Christianity for neglecting the values of the censors and the beauty of the human body and its movement.[14]

No pastor who cares about evangelism and discipleship in this culture can read those words without soberly considering how the church might reclaim its rightful place as the preeminent patron of the arts. There is much in our culture that is beautiful and profound, waiting to be liberated so it can lift its song to the Creator. Let us be willing to take the risks that allow beauty to triumph over the beast.

•

## CHAPTER ELEVEN

# PLANNING

## *The Myth of Spontaneity*

—◊◊◊—

*Care for detail in worship is not a search for perfectionism,*
*but an awareness that every part contributes to the whole.*
—Ruth C. Duck

### SILVER BULLET

Having a thoughtfully planned structure makes
worship services flow naturally.

Having been raised in a revivalistic tradition that viewed the ideal worship service as something like a camp-meeting rally, I was well into ministerial life before I began to think seriously about my role as a worship planner. I'd been taught that to plan worship was to handcuff the Holy Spirit. Real worship, I'd always heard, is spontaneous. This was the rationale behind having no printed order of service in our churches and was, I now suspect, the reason our worship services typically fell into the predictable rut of three hymns and an offering followed by three points and a poem. I don't think anyone blamed *that* on the Holy Spirit.

With the worship renewal movement has come the much-needed understanding that planning worship does not supplant the Spirit's role. In fact, to engage in the ministry of worship planning prayerfully, in submission to the Spirit himself, is a testament of our devotion to Him. Ultimately, nothing can supplant what the Spirit does in worship. Yet more often than not, He chooses to work through the vehicles—hymns, liturgy, sermons—that we have provided precisely for that purpose.

And what, exactly, would it mean to be spontaneous in worship? From a survey of biblical history, we might conclude that spontaneous worship is the sort of thing that gets people killed! In the excitement of the moment, Aaron's sons, Nadab and Abihu, acted spontaneously—and thoughtlessly—in worship. They offered "strange fire" to the Lord. By doing so, they were disobedient, and they paid a terrible price. Whatever spontaneity in worship means, it does not include doing whatever strikes one's fancy. From the beginnings of Israel's worship, God prescribed certain ways, or rites, through which the people could approach Him. Modern worship renewal has, in most cases, allowed for the spontaneity of the Spirit in the midst of carefully organized worship. In fact, the more contemporary and free-flowing worship is, the more planning that may be necessary.

That is why truly spontaneous worship is a myth. Whenever we enter God's presence, it must be done thoughtfully, with the intention to adore and obey Him. That doesn't mean that *we* are responsible for—or capable of—making worship meaningful. As Thomas Long reminds us, worship is meaningful already.[1] We don't plan worship services in order to make them valuable to God. We plan worship as an expression of our sincerity in approaching Him. It is precisely because we love God and see Him as worthy of our best that we take the discipline of planning worship seriously. To plan a service that flows seamlessly from beginning to end, centered on a unifying theme, is to offer up something agreeable to God, "an aroma, well pleasing to the Lord."

Carelessness in planning worship creates a nearly insurmountable barrier for people at a cost only God knows for sure. Thoughtless acts such as making poor choices about music, being insensitive to the local time frame of the service, and even asking congregants to stand or remain seated for too long can hinder people from entering into worship. While it is impossible to please all the people all the time—and that is not the aim of worship anyway—it is vital that the service itself not become a barricade against true worship.

Worship planning is a vital task. If we are to lead people before God each Sunday, then we must master the content, structure, and style of worship as well as have some command of its essential ingredients. By doing so, we can create worship events that honor God, have biblical and theological integrity, and accurately reflect the ethos and traditions of our local congregations.

## THE CONTENT OF WORSHIP

There is no single biblical pattern for worship; there are a variety of ways in which people may come before God. Yet within that diversity of expression, there can be no variety in content. The content of worship, as Robert Webber has put it, must always be the story of God's redemptive acts, especially in Jesus Christ. This is what worship is about.

While on vacation one year, I happened to attend church on the Fourth of July. Instead of a worship service, I witnessed a patriotic rally, complete with flag waving and political speeches. Prayer and Scripture were used less to celebrate God's redemptive work than to advance a cause. That phenomenon is not uncommon, and nationalism is not the only intruder in the sanctuary. We frequently insert some agenda into worship besides the celebration of God's saving work. Our concerns vary with the tide of our culture. Today, the issues of personal finances and national interest frequently displace our focus on God. A decade ago our concern was for motherhood and the family. Before that it was the institutional growth of the church.

But worship is about God, period.

Whenever the psalms praise God, for example, they praise Him for some reason—because of what He has done or will do. The acts of God are the proper focus of our worship. Nothing should be allowed to replace that content in our services—not our feelings, our ambition to build buildings, or, worst of all, a review of *our* acts of righteousness. It is God's redemptive work that we celebrate. The content of worship is nonnegotiable.

Worship planners who follow the lectionary are perhaps more likely to keep their worship rooted in the story of Scripture and less likely to insert their own agenda or a current cultural concern into the worship service. Whether by that means or some other, the content of worship must be fixed on God's redemptive work. We tell His story, not our own.

## THE STRUCTURE OF WORSHIP

If God is the object of our worship and if His saving acts are its content, then we must find some way to present this content to the people. This is the question of structure. Webber notes that there has been a fourfold pattern of worship evident throughout most of the church's history.[2] It is a pattern that offers a framework for worship planning in nearly any context.

- We gather.
- We hear God speak.
- We respond to God's Word.
- We dismiss.

While there has always been—and will continue to be—variety in the way these elements are observed, the basic pattern is nearly always evident in authentic worship. These are the four pillars upon which a worship service is built.

### GATHERING

The church—as the *ecclesia*, the called-out assembly—gathers for the purpose of worshiping God. Public worship must have some starting point, and the purpose of *gathering* as an element of worship is to bring the assembly together so that it may corporately enter into worship. There are a host of methods that can be employed to gather the church, including preludes, choral introits, congregational calls to worship (spoken or sung), invocations, and other prayers. Most worship planners, however, undervalue this element of the service. Too often, the service begins abruptly or without concern for the immediate context—what people are experiencing at the moment worship begins. Families arrive at church on Sunday morning in harried condition. Children have been made to brush their teeth and bathe against their will. Spouses have bickered. Teenagers are bored and distracted. Few people arrive at church ready to worship. As pastors, we have been eating, sleeping, and dreaming about the service for most of the week. But no one else has. Most members of the congregation have not invested themselves emotionally and spiritually in preparing for an encounter with God. They need to be gathered, brought together, so they may worship.

And that's likely to take some time. The idea that hearing a prelude or reciting one or two lines of a call to worship will prime the average churchgoer for worship is disingenuous. It takes effort to focus the attention of a body of people. A pastor must know his or her people well enough to perceive what will truly gather them—and to judge when they have arrived at the point of togetherness. This is one reason the modern worship renewal movement has placed an emphasis on congregational singing at the beginning of worship. It is a gathering mechanism. It calls people together, calls them to worship.

When people have been properly gathered, they hear the Word of God in a manner and to a degree that simply isn't possible when they are not well prepared. Good church musicians are masters at gathering the people, calling them to come and give themselves to the worship of God. The underemphasis of this element of structure hamstrings worship from the outset. No worship service will reach its true potential when the people are not adequately brought into God's presence.

## HEARING

The second aspect of our fourfold structure involves hearing God speak. The worship of Israel was characterized by attention to the Word of God. This reminds us that Scripture should have a central place in Christian worship. Obviously, this is where the sermon or homily fits liturgically, but there is more to hearing God speak than listening to the pastor. The public reading of Scripture has been part of the Judeo-Christian tradition from at least as far back in history as the formation of the synagogue in the postexilic period. Scripture, in a variety of forms, should be a prominent part of our services. Evangelicals typically claim the highest view of Scripture but often use it the least in public worship. Are we shamed by that fact?

Correcting the situation will require more than simply adding multiple Scripture readings to the order of worship, although that would be a good start. Emphasizing the hearing of the Word means looking for ways to allow God to speak to the gathered assembly under the auspices of His Word. That can include selecting hymn texts that are based on Scripture, employing various kinds of Scripture reading such as choral or dramatic reading, drama, and even visual art.

Some time ago I was guest preacher in a worship service during which a psalm of Creation was read. During the reading, the words of the psalm were projected before the congregation against a breathtaking backdrop of nature photographs. The effect was stunning; the congregation truly heard the Word of God. Worship planners who follow the lectionary have the advantage of having passages from the Psalms, Old Testament, New Testament, and Gospels thoughtfully selected for them. Those texts may be presented either in their entirety or selectively. Whether by that means or some other, a challenge for worship planners is to creatively engage the gathered people in hearing God through His Word.

## RESPONDING

Hearing God speak obligates us to make some response. The most desirable response is submission to God, which results in obedience. The clearest example of this kind of response, and the one used universally by the church, is the Eucharist, or Lord's Supper. This expression of thanksgiving to God for His gracious invitation to us in Christ is the most powerful symbol we have of what it means to respond to God in faith. Happily, the Lord's Supper is now observed more frequently in churches that used to celebrate it only quarterly or annually. I believe that the prominence of the Eucharist has been a major factor in the recent renewal of worship in the church. Monthly, even weekly, Eucharistic services are not uncommon in evangelical churches these days. This is a positive development in the liturgical life of the church.

There are other ways of responding to God in worship. In the revivalistic tradition in which I was raised, the altar call served as the invitation for people to respond to what God had said to them. While public invitations of that kind are becoming rarer, there are a number of other ways in which people can be invited to make a tangible response to God in worship. The presentation of tithes and offerings can be made as a response to God. I often deliberately place the offering late in the order of worship to use it as an occasion for teaching people that giving to God from our material means is a symbol of the greater offering of our whole selves. Singing hymns or songs that address God, especially if the lyrics capture the theme of the sermon or Scripture, can help people respond to God's Word. Sacraments and rituals such as baptism, the reception of members, covenants, the renewal of vows, and writing also call people to respond to God based on what His Spirit has said to them.

## DISMISSING

The fourfold pattern of worship is brought to completion through the dismissal, or scattering, of the church. The church has been gathered to worship corporately in a setting that edifies the body and bears witness to the world. But the church does not remain in that gathered state. It is dismissed, it is scattered, it is sent into the world. The motto "Enter to worship; depart to serve" is often placed prominently in church buildings, and that is theologically appropriate. The congregation must be dismissed to undertake its mission in the world.

Dismissing the church properly enables people to grasp their calling, which is to *be* the church in the world during the coming week. Benedictions, or blessings, play an important part in this stage of worship and must be chosen with care. Typically, pastors give little thought to this element of worship structure. Often, the closing words in the worship service are announcements for the day or program reminders for the coming week. Benedictions, when given, may be selected thoughtlessly.

Some pastoral theologians suggest that this is precisely where public announcements do belong. They do, after all, have to do with the work of the church in the world. Yet by this point in the worship service, the average congregant has mentally departed. If announcements are to be made at this point, it must be done carefully and will probably involve educating the congregation about the reason for placing these reminders at this point. The words that conclude a worship service should do more than announce the end. They should signal the beginning of the weeklong experience of being God's people in the world.

This fourfold structure of gathering, hearing, responding, and dismissing is not a straightjacket for worship planners. It is a skeleton that supports the animation of worship. People don't care to see a skeleton; it is the body that interests them. That is true of worship also. Good liturgy does not call attention to itself but is always present. It is the structure that supports worship. While most congregations probably under- or overemphasize a particular aspect of worship, evangelicals in general seem prone to neglecting the gathering and dismissing elements of liturgy. Each of the four pillars must be present to support a balanced experience of worship on Sunday mornings.

## THE STYLE OF WORSHIP

Worship style, as Webber puts it, is the atmosphere in which the content and structure of worship are played out.[3] We turn to matters of style last and not first in our discussion, and the order is imperative. Only after determining the content of worship and the structure through which it will be presented can the question of style be answered. Many who are tasked with the planning worship want to begin with style—especially the style of music. Over the years, I have frustrated more than one church member with my consistent unwillingness to talk about stylistic issues until first settling the questions of content and structure.

Yet style is not trivial; it is an essential aspect of worship planning. Webber gets at the importance of style this way:

> While the content of worship (the gospel) is non-negotiable, and the fourfold pattern of worship is strongly recommended, the style of worship is subject to considerable variety. This is because worshiping styles are rooted in the ever-changing kaleidoscope of human culture. There is no one style of worship that is suitable for all people always and everywhere, instead the style of worship will differ according to time and place, relative to the changing patterns of culture.[4]

This is good news for pastors, worship leaders, and all those with a hand in planning worship because it reminds us that while the content of worship is fixed and its structure is well established, there are still any number of ways to proceed from there. We can adapt to a changing context without compromising the integrity of worship by adjusting matters of style.

### INCORPORATING STYLISTIC WORSHIP

Style in worship is mostly a matter of preference. I say mostly because the propriety of a worship style for a given context is always important. Yet if the content and structure of worship are properly determined, a pastor can safely render that worship plan in the style that best suits his or her congregation. The style of worship—from high liturgy to low church, from traditional to contemporary—is nowhere prescribed in Scripture. Our job as worship planners is to center worship around the gospel, structured in a way that properly gathers, proclaims, invites, and dismisses, all in a style that best communicates to a particular church body. If those planning worship are truly in touch with the congregation, are wholly committed to God, and are ardent in their desire to lead people in authentic worship, questions of style will always be secondary. Primary concerns will be the glory and majesty of God and His saving acts toward humankind. More important than musical styles will be the manner in which worship enables people to freely enter into saving intimacy with God.[5]

Once these priorities are properly ordered, the task of planning worship becomes one of finding appropriate ways to develop a unified theme throughout the service. The failure to identify a particular service's theme (that is, to determine the particular content) can easily doom the liturgy to aiming at everything and hitting nothing. The worship planners task is to construct a service that thoughtfully remains close to the day's theme in a way that allows the congregation to see the bigger liturgical picture. It goes without saying that some services will be better done, or more obvious in terms of theme, than will others. But worship planners must always make an honest attempt to keep the liturgy headed in essentially the same direction and not be pulled off course by matters of style—items with cultural relevance but no real significance in celebrating the work of God among us.

## CHAPTER TWELVE

# ELEMENTS

## *Six Smooth Stones for Worship Leaders*

—⟋ɯ⟍—

*The liturgy itself is a country we must learn to dwell in. It contains many languages and customs that form a crucible of experience, a multi-layered culture, if you will.*
—Don Saliers

### SILVER BULLET
The careful selection of liturgical elements transforms a service from mundane to meaningful.

In an earlier chapter, I revealed my terror as a new pastor regarding the task of putting together an order of worship. That was much more daunting to me than was the task of preaching itself. I suspect this is rather common in church life, and accounts for why so many pastors are so willing to cede this responsibility to others—even those less qualified for the task than the pastor him- or herself.

After awhile, however, I got over my apprehension and began to enjoy the opportunity to be creative with public worship. Those early experiences were salted by failure. Yet thanks to a patient congregation with a healthy sense of humor, I can look back on those early days as mostly positive. Probably the most critical discovery I made as a young worship planner was to stumble across certain essential ingredients, or focal points as I call them, for planning worship. Paying attention to these six focal points does not guarantee that Sunday's worship will be explosive. But ignoring them makes it pretty close to a lead-pipe cinch that the day will be fraught with problems.

## ONE: PROPER AND ORDINARY ELEMENTS

A *proper element* of liturgy is something in the order of service that is proper for the occasion. During the season of Advent, many churches use an Advent wreath as an element of worship. This is a proper element because it is used only during Advent. On the other hand, almost every congregation takes an offering every week. The offering is an *ordinary element* of the liturgy. Other items such as prayer, Bible readings, and singing are ordinary elements as well.

By paying attention to the Christian year, it is relatively easy to know which *propers*, as they are called, ought to be employed on a given Sunday. There may be other special occasions in the life of the church, things like anniversaries and local celebrations, that call for proper elements that would make sense only to that particular congregation. By identifying and differentiating these elements, a worship planner can then decide how each should be used in the service—where it best fits and how much attention it should be given.

In regard to ordinary elements, the challenge is to find ways to prevent them from becoming too ordinary so that people don't take them for granted. Two of these ordinary elements are in particular need of being rescued from mundanity: the offering and prayer.

### OFFERING

Many congregations are sensitive—perhaps overly so—to the culture's perception regarding the church and money. In addressing this cultural mistrust, some worship planners have gone so far as to delete the offering from the order of worship. That is a significant mistake for at least two reasons. First, it is an overreaction to a criticism that can be addressed by less drastic means. Being good managers of money, supporting one's community in visible ways, and being completely candid about finances will change the public's perception without endangering the church budget. Second, and more important, worship itself is a series of offerings. We offer ourselves bodily present before God in a particular locale. We offer our voices to God as the most obvious way of combining mind, body, and will. And we offer something of our material wealth as a symbol of the greater gift of ourselves. One of the reasons the offering has become a sort of intermission in so many churches is that pastors have failed to teach the significance of giving gifts to God. The offering is the epitome of a teachable moment, one in which people can be urged to give cheerfully to God as a way of expressing their devotion to Him.

## PRAYER

At its best, prayer offered in worship can be such a holy moment that removing one's shoes would seem entirely fitting. At its worst, prayer can become the liturgical equivalent of charades, a parlor game in which the actor communicates hilariously through indirect means. What passes for prayer in public worship is often something else mislabeled as communication with God.

*Announcement.* Every churchgoer has had the misfortune of listening to a worship leader who was ostensibly talking to God but in reality making announcements to the congregation. "Oh Lord, bless the youth gathering that will begin at 7:00 p.m. in the fellowship hall, immediately following the service." Announcements are a legitimate part of a public worship service. They underscore the reality of the body of Christ in everyday life. There's no need to apologize for them. At the same time they are not the proper content of prayer.

*Segue.* Although I normally keep my eyes closed during times of corporate prayer, as a teacher of worship, I peek once in awhile purely for research purposes. Often, my suspicion is confirmed that a "prayer" is being used to cover the exit of people from the chancel or to set up the next part of the service. To misuse prayer in that way sends a harmful message to those who are peeking with no research motivation. It tells them that prayer is a trivial exercise, akin to a television timeout during a football game.

*Coercion.* Sadly, prayer is sometimes used to create a mood during the worship service or to manipulate the emotions of those attending. This may be done unintentionally through the habitual use of background music during prayer. Worshipers may be conditioned to associate prayerfulness with certain emotive responses.

*Tradition.* In many churches, prayer is practiced just because— because we've always done it, because this is what you do at this point in the service, because it's a tradition. Prayer of this type trivializes the exercise and does a disservice to worshipers who, now more than ever, need to be taught the value of prayer and need to have it modeled so they clearly see its significance to the Christian life.

*Recapitulation.* This abuse of prayer is done mostly by preachers who take the opportunity to repreach their sermon. As pastors, we get one shot at communicating with the congregation each week. If twenty minutes is not enough time to accomplish the task, another three minutes won't get the point across.

*Monologue.* Prayer, rather than being addressed to God, is sometimes addressed to those in attendance. It can degenerate into a monologue. Must public prayer always be made by one person who speaks aloud while others either struggle to listen or allow their minds to wander aimlessly? There are ways to make public prayer more participatory, and thoughtful worship planners employ them. This does not mean the tradition of the pastoral prayer should be discontinued. It simply means that prayer in worship is for everyone, and we must find ways to meaningfully involve the congregation in the prayer life of the church during worship.

*Speech.* Our conception of prayer is that it must always involve speaking. That is not the case. In previous chapters, I've confessed my preference for the inclusion of silence in worship. I have been powerfully moved to pray during worship services by the meaningful use of silence. The older I grow in the faith, the more I find my own experience of prayer inclined toward listening rather than speaking. Thoughtful worship planners will allow opportunities for this. Hymns, songs, and Scripture passages may also be used as prayers. Prayer can be something other than a spoken word.

*Absent.* It's both surprising and frightening to consider how little the modern church prays in public worship. While Evangelicals are fond of criticizing mainline and Catholic worship as dry and formal, those services are filled with prayer. Evangelical worship moves at an almost breathless pace with little or no time devoted to prayer. This can be especially true where the object of the service is to make worship accessible to seekers. Elements of worship that may be unfamiliar to the unchurched or evoke bad memories for the dechurched are excluded. As a result, prayer is either absent or is minimized in the order of worship. The early church, on the other hand, understood liturgy itself mostly in terms of prayer.

Our penchant for reducing the place of prayer in worship is at odds with even our own culture. Survey after survey has shown that most people, even those who don't consider themselves religious, pray regularly. It is odd, therefore, that we so often leave prayer out of our worship services.

## PASTORAL PRAYER

Some years ago I visited a large church where the pastor was highly regarded. I had heard the man preach in another setting and immediately realized preaching was not his gift. I wondered what accounted for his reputation as a pastor. When I heard him pray during the morning worship service, I had all the answer I needed. This was a pastor who took his calling to the priesthood very seriously. He mediated between God and the people in a way that I have seldom witnessed before or since. Too often, pastors wing it during the pastoral prayer because they attach little importance to their priestly role. Liturgical scholar James White writes,

> The chief problem with the pastoral prayer is that it often tries to do everything, and often ends by doing nothing. At its best, it can be a magnificent articulation of the congregation's deepest feelings and needs. Too often, the pastoral prayer is simply overloaded, it tries to cover confession, thanksgiving, intercession and all points between, as if one try were better than several.[1]

To add weight to this element of worship, try writing out a pastoral prayer, even if you typically pray spontaneously. Writing prayers brings focus and clarity, allowing the pastor to incorporate a theme into the pastoral prayer, especially the theme of that day's worship. While prayer, liturgically speaking, is an ordinary element, it is always properly included in worship and can be the means of extraordinary movement by God in the lives of people.

## Two: Propriety

A second focal point in planning worship is propriety, meaning the cultural fit of the worship elements and the congregation, denominational distinctives, and the general suitability of any element within the liturgy. An earlier chapter mentioned the church's need to acculturate the gospel by representing the best aspects of local culture in worship. Ruth Duck writes that "to incarnate the gospel in worship means to express the central meanings of the service in culturally appropriate forms. To insert cultural elements that are unrelated to the rest of worship fails to honor either the culture or the experience of worship."[2] But a caution is necessary here. Being clever culturally is not appropriate in worship. From the 1970s to the present I have endured countless tortured renditions of Simon and Garfunkel's "Bridge Over Troubled Water" in church services under the guise of cultural adaptation—Jesus is the bridge, get it?—that I am leery of attempts to bring pop culture to church. Still, we can find ways to bridge the culture around us.

Propriety is a guiding principle in particular for the selection of music and for determining which proper elements of worship would be most effective for a local church. For example, the decision as to how prominently to emphasize the Christian calendar could well depend on the way a congregation has been taught to think about such matters. For some churches unfamiliar with this way of keeping liturgical time adoption of the church year might be an easy transition. Yet for others, the church calendar may seem overly formal and, therefore, void of meaning. Some attempts at creative liturgy fail not because they are bad ideas but because they were poorly timed—they lacked propriety. Congregations must be educated before they will embrace new forms of liturgy. Pastors who violate that sense of proper timing do so at their own risk.

## THREE: PARTICIPATION

A third focal point in worship planning is participation. In a previous chapter, we noted that good liturgy is that which includes the participation of the people—ideally, all of them. A marked lack of participation may be the single greatest failure in today's worship services. And the failure happens at both ends of the style spectrum. In higher, or more formal, kinds of worship, people may be overwhelmed by the sound of a pipe organ, a liturgy they do not understand, or a missal they cannot follow. In new, less formal, worship, participants may be left behind because they do not know the music or are unable to follow the worship leader. In both cases the result is passivity among worshipers, and the chances of reengaging their attention once lost are slim. Leaders must keep a close eye on the likelihood of gaining participation when planning any element of worship. What is being asked of the people? Can they do it? Are they likely to be willing? Are there enough participative elements to keep them engaged? How are these pieces of the liturgy spaced throughout the service? Singing for thirty minutes followed by thirty minutes of listening is a recipe for passive worship. Worship is for the people; therefore, its effectiveness is not judged by musical aesthetics or by the quality of performance by the leaders. Worship's value is gauged by the participation (the liturgy) of the congregation.

## FOUR: POSITION

A fourth element that ought to be carefully monitored in planning worship is position, or what has been called the vertical-to-horizontal axis. Worship is a multi-relational event. It concerns the vertical relationship between God and the worshipers, but it also involves the horizontal relationships between the worshipers themselves. While the preponderance of liturgical acts are oriented vertically, there are, nonetheless, vital aspects of worship that clearly move the axis of the service to the horizontal plane. This is one reason why, for example, making announcements during a worship service tends to be troublesome. Making announcements is both necessary and theologically significant in that it points to the reality of the faith community. Yet it orients the service almost exclusively in the horizontal direction. For this reason, worship planners must place the announcements carefully. In most worship services, the axis can be moved between vertical and horizontal a couple of times at most. Any more, and the service begins to unravel. I have attended worship services in which there was a strong vertical alignment following a particularly powerful musical presentation, but that was undone by a sharp horizontal turn—an appeal for nursery workers. In some cases, this U-turn can't be helped, so we smile about it and do the best we can. On other occasions we have no one to blame but ourselves for the poor planning that hijacked the alignment of the service. As worship planners, we must pay attention to the direction of the liturgy, being careful not to move it back and forth too often. To do so will frustrate the people and, ultimately, tarnish the credibility of the worship leader.

## FIVE: PROPORTIONALITY

The fifth focal point for worship planners is proportionality. A sense of balance is important for art in any medium, and the art of worship is no different. There must be balance between the elements of the service, and appropriate movement from one to the next.

Most preachers know what it's like to be involved in a service that lacks proportionality so that they have to edit their sermon on the fly to correct the imbalance. That's a miserable experience, and all the worse when we have no one to blame but ourselves for the disproportional construction of the event. In a previous day, the tendency was for services to be disproportional in their overemphasis on preaching. In a previous chapter, I mentioned some ways in which preaching can be adapted to liturgical practice. The current emphasis on music in worship has created a tendency to become disproportional by neglecting other kinds of liturgical practice. Correcting the imbalance does not mean that every detail of the service must be obsessively managed. Yet those planning worship must steward the time they are given as best they can, following through on the thematic content for that day in a manner that creates symmetry and balance.

## SIX: PROGRESSION

Finally, worship planners need to be mindful of the progression of the services they are constructing. Progression is the pace or flow of a worship service. Most services will have a climactic point toward which the service builds. Whether that be the proclamation of the Word, the response to the proclamation, the Eucharist, or something else, the service should be structured in a way that the congregation makes the journey to that climactic point without becoming fatigued, confused, or apathetic. Generally, that is accomplished by placing acts of worship that have the same function together. For example, preaching and the reading of Scripture both concern proclamation, so they are naturally placed together. Giving and serving have a common element, so the announcements might logically be placed near the offering. When a service has good progression, the congregation can follow the order, whether it is written or not. They will have a sense that one element of the liturgy leads naturally into another. When an element is placed into the order of worship haphazardly, simply because it needs to be done during the service, people become confused and their attention wanders.

In spite of our current emphasis on spontaneity in worship, most people, especially those unfamiliar with the church, prefer to have some sense of where things are going in a worship service. Designing a service that has both a recognizable destination and the requisite elements to get there will gain the trust and confidence of the congregation.

Pace is a vital aspect of a service's progression. Many worship services are cluttered with elements and move far too quickly from one to the next. Worship is not a race! A fundamental conviction that should guide all worship planning is this: Less is more. Simplicity in the order of worship is always to be preferred over sensory overload. If there are gaps in the service, allow the Spirit of God to fill them—not unnecessary words from the pastor or worship leader. Worship should be characterized by peace, rest, and clarity, not frenetic activity that leaves one worn out.

Giving due attention to these six focal points will not, by itself, produce a vital worshiping community. But the chances of enabling people to authentically connect with God are much more promising when informed, sincere, and prayerful planning has been done around these elements. Planning worship services that are unified in theme, participative in liturgical style, and balanced and symmetrical comes from weekly practice. On some Sundays it seems as if heaven has opened, and it is tempting to believe that "I can do this now." Yet there will always be a great deal of mystery in worship because it is an encounter with God himself. And even on those Sundays when it seems that nothing has gone as planned, God is present, wishing to be found by those who truly seek Him. The important factor for those of us responsible for constructing and leading services that create that divine encounter is that we honestly and wholeheartedly give ourselves to the task. Our skill will improve with time. And in the meantime, we lift our efforts before God as yet another offering to Him.

## CHAPTER THIRTEEN

# MISSION

## *The Transforming Power of Worship*

—ᴍ—

*The test of our worship becomes our fidelity to the call to
follow Jesus, not simply our success in admiring Jesus.*
—William Willimon

### SILVER BULLET

When worship becomes a weeklong activity and not a
Sunday ritual, it will transform the community.

It is known in popular parlance as *quality time*. That term expresses
the idea that a single hour in which one's full attention is given to
some pursuit or person is inherently more valuable than any larger
quantity of time in which one's mind is less intensively engaged. It is
true that there are some circumstances in which that notion makes
sense. My wife, for example, values having my undivided attention
for thirty minutes more than having my mere physical presence at
home for three hours—unless those hours are spent doing housework!
But in our Day-Timer–driven daily lives, we have come to use the
notion of quality time as a pretext for rationalizing our inability or
unwillingness to reorder our priorities around the things that matter
most. So today's overcommitted parents spend "quality time" with
their overscheduled kids, hoping an hour at Chuck E. Cheese's will

make up for a week of virtual isolation. The problem is that while kids know how to count, they do not know how to evaluate. They want more of our time, not more of our undivided attention. An hour a week of "quality time" will not sustain a healthy family life, nor was it ever meant to.

In the same way, worship cannot be a one-hour-a-week event for a healthy Christian. Christian faith is a relationship that will radically transform every aspect of human life. That's an ambitious agenda, to say the least. At the center of this lifelong transformation stands worship—the adoration of God and submission to Him. While true worship begins with the redemption and restoration of a human being to fellowship with God, that is not the end of the story, nor was it ever intended to be. Salvation brings a person into a transforming worship relationship with the Creator. That worship relationship stands behind God's salvific acts on our behalf. When we choose to humbly submit to Him, learn His ways, and obediently serve Him, our lives will be transformed, lock, stock, and Visa card. Such is the power of worship. Yet that power can be subverted by limiting worship to the "quality time" of one hour on Sunday.

In an earlier chapter, we identified barriers to true worship, including ritualism, which divorces worship from the remainder of life. It is precisely this attempt to compartmentalize life into neat categories leads us to apply the notion of quality time to the Christian faith. Whatever else we might conclude about such an approach, we can be confident that it will not produce life transformation. David Peterson writes,

> Worship in the New Testament is a comprehensive category describing the Christian's total existence. It is co-extensive with the faith—response wherever and whenever that response is elicited. Consequently, our traditional understanding of worship as restricted to the cult of gathering or the congregation at a designated time and place for rite and

proclamation will no longer do. This is not what the New Testament means by worship.[1]

Biblically, the matter is clear: Worship never ends at noon. The benediction does not terminate our need for worship any more than paying a restaurant check signals the end of our hunger for more than a few hours. Real worship influences us in such a way that we become perpetual worshipers. Thomas Long has it right when he says, "Worship is a soundtrack for the rest of life, the words, and music, and actions of worship inside the sanctuary playing in the background of our lives outside, in the world."[2]

## FULL-SIZE WORSHIP

When Paul writes in Romans 12 that our fundamental response to God should be to offer our entire lives, including our bodies, as living sacrifices, the apostle calls us to a comprehensive view of worship in human life. He had in mind our everyday lives, not merely a block of time on Sunday morning. This is the same apostle who admonished us, "Whatever you do, in word or deed, do everything in the name of the Lord Jesus, giving thanks to God the Father through him" (Col. 3:17 RSV). This is the language of worship used in conjunction with real life. Peterson says, "Fundamentally then, worship in the New Testament means believing the gospel and responding with one's whole life and being to the person of God's Son in the power of the Holy Spirit . . . The whole of life is to be lived in relation to the cross and to the extent to which Christ is enthroned as our crucified Savior and High Priest."[3] Living all of one's days in the shadow of the Cross and in gratitude to God is precisely how the transforming power of worship is unleashed in our lives. Jesus himself quoted the prophets in drawing an unmistakable line connecting worship and obedient living: "This people honors me with their lips, but their heart is far from me" (Mark 7:6; Isa. 29:13 RSV). This underscores the fact that worship is faith expressed in obedience and adoration *in all of life*. To relegate worship to Sunday only is to subvert God's redemptive intention to transform our lives.

This is a call to see worship in its larger context. If pastors want to revitalize the worship of the church, they must begin to revitalize the worshipers. This is accomplished by calling people to view life— every aspect of it—as a response to God. That's what worship is, our fitting response to who God is and what He has done for us. Scripture teaches that even as God's love attends us wherever we go, so should our praise continually ascend to Him. This is worship extended to its full size—encompassing all of life.

## WORSHIP AND ETHICS

Limiting our response to God to the time spent in a particular building or in doing acts that are mostly unlike anything we do the rest of the week is not at all what Paul meant in urging us to make our lives a living sacrifice to God. When we limit worship in that way, it nearly always results in a disconnect between professed faith and behavior. The well-publicized televangelism scandals of the 1980s bear painful witness to the incongruity of professing to love God while living outside the bounds of His will.

The necessary connection between worship and ethics must be emphasized in modern church life because of the pervasive tendency to divide life into unrelated segments. No amount of passion and intensity on Sunday mornings, corporate or individual, can atone for willful and unconfessed sin committed throughout the week. God desires—yea, expects—to be honored in all of life, not just in the church sanctuary. Israel's problems in the Old Testament had their root in the notion that so long as Temple worship was carried out appropriately, people could live as they chose. The writings of the prophets offer poignant testimony as to how mistaken those ancient worshipers were. We are equally mistaken in thinking that the quality or intensity of our Sunday worship will cover our workday disobedience. "In worship we received the self-giving love of God and the test of our thankfulness is whether we reproduce that pattern of self-giving in our daily relationships with other people."[4]

## WORSHIP AND MISSION

When our lives bear witness to God's existence in ways that catch the attention of unbelievers, then the church accomplishes its mission to be light and salt to the world. For that to happen, Christians must be willing to leave the church building and *be* the church in the world. To make that possible, our worship services must reinforce Scripture's teaching on the mission of the church and every believer's part in it. When we gather on Sundays to worship, that corporate event must be seen as a prelude to being dismissed, or scattered, to go forth and be the church wherever we may find ourselves. Long writes,

> The connections between Sunday worship and the workaday week are far more subtle and complex than quoting Scripture at dinner parties, whistling hymns at Little League games, or reading Paul's epistles at business conferences. What we need is to discover how the dinner party, the Little League game, the business meeting, and all other aspects of our Monday-to-Saturday world are already present in worship, woven into the very fabric of prayer, hymn, and sermon.[5]

Presenting ourselves, our whole selves, to God in worship on Sundays necessarily includes the offering of our workplaces, homes, and recreation sites to Him as well. Pastors should remind worshipers of this, with the expectation that they will leave the church building prepared to continue their witness to God's sovereign authority and abiding interest in our lives regardless of what they may be doing.

What you hear whispered, Jesus told His followers, proclaim from the housetops (Matt. 10:27). Jesus tells us that what we hear privately in worship we should also discuss openly in our work, our political activities, and in our civic life. We take our cues about what we say to those outside the church from what is said inside it—in worship.[6]

## WORSHIP AND POWER

Pastors who are concerned about the reticence or refusal of their people to bear witness to the faith should begin to address the problem by examining the content of the church's worship. Jesus said that a city set on a hill cannot be hidden (Matt. 5:14). The purpose of light is to illuminate, and nothing should increase the "candle power" of the church so much as the worship and adoration of God. Whether the metaphor is light, salt, or leaven, the intention is clear: Worship is meant to strengthen and enhance the witness of God's people in the world. The weakness, ineffectiveness, or absence of the church's witness indicates a disconnect between worship and life that must be mended. If it is not, the result will be worship that is perfunctory and, ultimately, powerless. In such cases, no amount of tinkering with the order of service or learning new music will suffice. What is needed is revival, a definite movement of God's Spirit upon people whose hearts have grown cold.

A. W. Tozer said, "The shallowness of our inner experience, the hollowness of our worship, and that servile imitation of the world which mocks our promotional methods all testify that we, in this day, know God only imperfectly, and the peace of God scarcely at all."[7] If the church's worship is not bringing its people into a deeper experience with God, the kind of experiences that spills over into the rest of their lives, then the church is failing at the very center of its calling.

## WORSHIP AND COMMUNITY RENEWAL

Bill Hybels, pastor of Willow Creek Community Church, has said that church is a beautiful thing—when it works right. Our world needs nothing more urgently than to have healthy churches functioning in vital and redemptive ways in its communities. Worship is one key to community renewal. The worship renewal that has swept this country is nothing less than the work of the Holy Spirit's trying to rouse a lethargic and ineffective church. This revitalized worship is not a new toy for the church. It is meant to be shared with the world. Often, Christians say things such as "Sunday worship helps me get through the week" or "Sundays are where I get my batteries recharged." While worship does benefit the believer, those who make such statements have missed half the point of worship. It is intended to transform both the Christian *and* the world.

Worship is reality therapy in the best sense of the term. It is where we retreat from a world that views what we do as escapism so that we may be infused with a true picture of who God is and who we are in relationship to Him. To come together with people of like faith and worship is to have our eyes adjusted so that we can go into the streets and tell others how the world looks from God's vantage point. To do less is to fail in our worship.

The traditional Catholic mass ends with these words, spoken by the deacon: "Go, you are dismissed," or, more literally, "Go, you are sent." The Latin word for *send* has the same root as the word for *mission*. So when we exit the worship service, we are missionaries sent out to be witnesses. We are to go and bear witness to God, whose Word we have encountered in worship. Where are we to go? To the world. And for most of us, the world is not a mission field in some distant land. It is an ordinary place we inhabit every week—a home, an office, a school. We are ordinary people, sharing what we have received in worship, loving people as we have been loved, forgiving as we have been forgiven.[8] It is as if the worship service never ends. Yes, it is a beautiful thing when it works right.

## CHAPTER FOURTEEN

# DISCIPLINES

## *Why Pastors Need Worship*

—━ᜒ━—

*What the church needs most is not another hymnal, a new sound system, a revised prayer book, or another set of published scripts. What the church needs most are discerning, prayerful, joyous people who treat their work as worship planners and leaders as a holy pastoral calling.*
—John D. Witvliet

### SILVER BULLET
Personal worship enhances a pastor's ability to lead others.

M ost of us who plan worship regularly are constantly searching for good ideas, songs, texts, scripts, and images—preferably before the end of the week—we can use to lead our congregations. But perhaps we are looking also for something deeper, something more than resources or techniques. Perhaps what we really need is a new way of conceptualizing our role as worship leaders that will sustain us in our day-to-day work with our congregations. This is especially true for battle-weary leaders. Many are burned out, worn to a frazzle from producing a full menu of services for weeks on end. Others are weary from working in congregations that are actively fighting the worship war or other church battles. Still others work tirelessly to lead worshipers who arrive with impossibly high expectations for others and few or none for themselves. In these situations, we need something more than techniques; we need a vision to encourage, sustain, and inspire us.[1]

My ideal, like that of many pastors, is that ministry ought to be the most joyful vocation in the world. And I have had my share of joyous days as a shepherd of God's flock. On many occasions I have been overwhelmed with gratitude for the privilege of being a midwife to someone's spiritual birth. At other times I've been overwhelmed by the power of the sermon text I was studying, amazed that people were willing to pay me to do something as enjoyable and life changing as preaching the Word of God. But I've had my share of those other moments as well, moments when driving a truck or selling insurance didn't sound so bad.

Origen, a church father from the third century, made an interesting comment on the prophetic call. While Isaiah cried out, "Here am I, Lord, send me!" Jonah found the first boat out of town. To Origen, Jonah's response was to be preferred because it was more realistic. The ancient father argued that those who too easily accept the call of God are not to be trusted. All who minister have had those what-was-I-thinking moments that serve to remind us how difficult this vocation can be.

Yet as pastors, the ministry is God's calling for our lives. So there must be a way to both flourish personally and be fit for the challenge of planning yet one more order of worship. This is Witvliet's "vision that can sustain." The task of leading worship is so critical to the health of the church that we must think about ways pastors keep themselves spiritually fit to do it. The place for pastors to begin is by worshiping themselves.

## PRACTICING SPIRITUAL DISCIPLINES

Sadly, many pastors are blind to their need for worship. Too often we are like physicians who have a lifesaving antidote and spend countless hours dispensing it to others but fail to take it themselves. We talk publicly about the importance of worship, the necessity of worship, and the restorative power of worship, and then spend the remainder of the service worrying about whether there are enough ushers for the offering. What pastor hasn't wasted precious mental energy before leading worship by taking a silent roll call to see who is present and who is absent on that Sunday?

Pastors must be worshipers, not just worship leaders. We must model for our people the proper approach to worship, providing for them an example to follow and not a mere order of service. Pastors who first worship personally will be far better equipped to lead others in the worship of God.

## SABBATH

When pastoral families are asked to name their least favorite day of the week, the winner, hands down, is Sunday. That's no surprise. It is a stress-filled, high-expectation, roller-coaster of a day that can leave one feeling like a prizefighter after a fifteen-round donnybrook. I have had some absolutely exhausting jobs in my life, including digging ditches and shoveling manure. None of those chores left me feeling the kind of fatigue I have felt on a Sunday evening after a more or less typical day in pastoral ministry. The fatigue associated with emotional and spiritual stress cannot be explained to those who have not experienced it. So even if a pastor enters into worship on Sundays with the congregation, that will not be the beside-still-waters experience for him or her that it might be for others. Something must supplement the corporate worship experience in order for the pastor to worship fully. So when does the pastor worship? Where can he or she go to get deep with God in spirit and truth? In other words, when and how does the pastor observe the Sabbath?

Sabbath-keeping by pastors is so important for the entirety of their pastoral ministry that it hardly seems fair to speak to this only in terms of their role as worship leaders. Yet after more than twenty years of pastoral experience including planning hundreds of worship services, I'm convinced that keeping one's own worship fresh and vital is the single most important step pastors can take both to provide for their own spiritual health and to provide vibrant worship experiences for their congregations. Practicing this spiritual discipline will pay dividends in the form of personal enthusiasm for corporate worship and a desire to see others experience a deep relationship with God in their lives as you have in your own. Crafting a particular strategy for spiritual formation is an individual task, yet certain classic disciplines have been particularly beneficial to those in the ministry. Silence and solitude are chief among them, disciplines that align themselves with Sabbath keeping. This is the intentional closeting of oneself away from noise and distractions in order to listen to God, to speak to Him from the heart, and to simply dwell in His presence. These two disciplines are indispensable for enabling pastors to rise above the inherent stressfulness of their vocation.

## SCRIPTURE

The study of Scripture is of paramount importance for ministry in general and for worship leading in particular. Studying God's Word in order to craft sermons that can hold up their end of the liturgical bargain is increasingly important for pastors. One benefit of this discipline is that it leads to the discovery of ways to connect Scripture with the rest of the liturgy. It is absolutely essential for pastors to give themselves wholeheartedly to the task of learning God's Word, both for their own spiritual health and for the well-being of their congregations. What could be more important for a spiritual shepherd to do than spend time in Scripture, listening to God speak and subsequently speaking to the congregation? Sadly, the study of Scripture is often the first item to be cut from the pastor's time budget. The congregation always pays for this in the long run.

Marva Dawn says that "the greatest weakness of much preaching is that the Word hasn't killed the pastor first."[2] The idea of the Word "killing" the preacher goes back to Martin Luther. The Reformers viewed the Word of God as the most powerful resource available to the minister. Anyone who flourishes in pastoral ministry over the long haul will be one who has been mortally wounded by the truth of Scripture. That experience, more so than formal training or any natural gifts, will bring vitality and depth to preaching that will spill over into the rest of the liturgy.

## STUDY

To be spiritually nourished and fit to lead worship, pastors must give themselves to aggressive reading regimens beyond the Bible, including resources in liturgical theology that can equip them for worship leadership. That includes everything from theology and church history to selected modern works of fiction, even film. Bringing the gospel to bear on the prevailing culture will require the pastor to have an adequate knowledge and understanding of that culture. The days where pastors can remain cloistered within the world of church and theology are over. The unpardonable sin for worship leaders in this age is to be so out of touch with the culture that people are never given an adequate view of the God who reigns over all cultures. Modern people are rejecting not the biblical God but an anachronistic stereotype of divinity. Pastors who devote themselves to being both spiritually fit and aware culturally will help to alleviate this common response to the faith.

Also, pastors need to keep current with what is happening in liturgical renewal. Incredible resources are available to pastors these days, an almost overwhelming array. Given the spate of books, periodicals, Web sites, software, and conferences and seminars devoted to worship, there is no reason why a pastor shouldn't be able to study the subject of worship for the benefit of his or her congregation.

## SERVICE

A final discipline important for worship planners is service. Given the fact that many pastors feel overworked and subject to unreasonably high expectations, it may seem surprising that the discipline of service would be suggested as a value for maintaining spiritual health. Yet in order to remain strong and vital leaders of worship, pastors will need to serve others. It is true that leading worship is a valuable service in its own right. Yet serving in other, less public ways helps leaders keep things in proper perspective and remember that caring for others is the kind of worship God always finds pleasing. Practicing the discipline of service helps pastors keep the horizontal dimension of worship in view.

In addition to keeping one's pastoral sanity intact and relationship with God vibrant, practicing the disciplines of Sabbath keeping, Scripture, study, and service will greatly enhance the pastor's creativity and discernment in constructing liturgy. As you deepen your own experience of God, you will gain new understanding of how to bring others into a closer relationship with Him. Marva Dawn puts the issue of pastoral spirituality in proper focus when she writes, "What visitors really seek in pastors is godliness . . . If pastors want the worship services over which they preside to reach out to nonmembers, the most important thing they can do is to nourish their own spiritual life."[3] At the end of the day, no liturgical gimmickry will make up for the shortcomings of a spiritually shallow shepherd. If you want to lead people in worship, you must first engage in worship yourself.

## SETTING PRIORITIES

Years ago I coached basketball at a small college in the Midwest. My mantra to the players was this: "You play like you practice." If Sunday worship is the "game," then our "play" as leaders will never rise above our practice of personal worship. The pastor's worship and spiritual habits are too important to be ignored. Yet no pastor has too few things on his or her to-do list. Adding (or enhancing) the disciplines mentioned in this chapter might seem overwhelming to pastors with already long job descriptions. So it is not more activities that are needed but right pastoral priorities.

The biggest factor in pastoral burnout is the frantic pace of pastoral life, fueled mostly by the unrealistic expectations of congregations and the willingness of pastors to adopt a business model of leadership. The old English term *curate* is perhaps the best descriptor of the pastoral vocation. A curate is a sort of physician of the soul. This is our business, to aid people in developing a healing relationship with God. Ordering our lives in such a way so that we ourselves can be healthy is not a waste of time—it should occupy the preponderance of ministry time. If the idea of maintaining the disciplines of Sabbath, Scripture, study, and service seems onerous, it is not the pastor's schedule but his or her priorities that need adjustment.

In his book *Worship Seeking Understanding*, John Witvliet constructs what he terms a profile for a worship leader.[4] Witvliet emphasizes three characteristics: a love of learning, a pastoral heart, and a spirit of joy. To be called to the role of leading God's people in worship is both a privilege and a responsibility. A lifetime love for learning about Scripture, liturgy, culture, and, especially, people is an indispensable aid to staying at the task for the long haul. A pastoral heart is bestowed by God and exemplified by the descriptive words of Christ himself in John 10, where Jesus contrasts the true shepherd with the hireling. Real shepherds don't run when the wolves attack. These days, they seem to attack most often in the area of worship, particularly worship music. That pastoral heart enables the pastor to explain yet again to that exasperated church member "why this church worships the way it does." The spirit of joy is likewise a gift from God, but it is a gift that can be cultivated and enhanced through one's own pursuit of God. Joy in the ministry is the reward for taking the long view of what truly matters in life. Joy is the end product of our own life of worship.

## CHAPTER FIFTEEN

# ESCHATOLOGY

## *Moving Worship Back to Its Future*

—⟋⟍—

*Christian worship is predicated on the understanding
that there is nothing left to achieve. It has already
been achieved, once and for all. The struggle is over;
the kingdom has been inaugurated and obtained.*
—James Alison

### SILVER BULLET

By focusing on long-term renewal rather than
short-term gain, pastors can elevate Sunday worship
to the high point of the church's week.

The sanctuary is empty now. A few cars remain in the parking lot, and small groups of people stand around to chat before heading home. As always, you're the last person to leave, having done the usual forty hours worth of administration, team building, and putting out of brush fires in the narthex—after leading God's people in worship. It's all in a Sunday's work for the pastor. You walk into your study, place your Bible and sermon notes on the desk along with various notes received during the morning. Before heading home, you pause, staring out the window. As you do every Sunday, you wonder, *What really happened here today? Did anyone listen to the sermon? Did people see the connections between the songs, the readings, and the message?* Eventually, you come to the real question that gnaws at your soul: *Does any of this really matter?*

The lowest point of a pastor's week is the time following the worship service. Many pastors experience an emotional crash on Sundays, regardless of how well the service went. The physical, spiritual, and emotional drain of leading people can leave one just this side of despair. We may look for responses from attendees by which to gauge the effectiveness of what we've done, but they are difficult to come by. People respond to worship in many different ways, most of them inward and beyond our best intuition. So we live with the pedestrian greetings at the rear of the church, punctuated now and again by a response from a person whose eyes betray the fact that he or she was genuinely moved by the service. If we're fortunate, there will be an e-mail or phone call that week from someone whose life was touched by worship. But these are oases in an otherwise arid desert of unknowing. Does our work matter? That question tests our faithfulness on a weekly basis. Thankfully, the answer is affirmative.

## TRANSFORMATION VERSUS SUCCESS

The effects of careful planning and leadership of worship are difficult to observe in the short term; but over the long run, they are much more readily seen. When watching plants grow in the garden, staring at them daily is pointless and agonizing. But after an absence of a few days, the effect of soil preparation, proper fertilization, and adequate watering is easily apparent. It is the same with leading worship. Pastors, of necessity, must be farsighted, willing to look beyond the immediate and see the cumulative effects of self-denying worship on the hearts and lives of people. That's the payoff for all those Sundays of staring out the window, battling haunting questions of meaning. Nothing in this life compares to seeing people grow deeper in their faith in God. Nothing can touch the exhilaration of seeing people break through their doubts and entrust themselves wholly to God. Remember that the next time you find yourself staring out the window, asking questions that mostly have to do with vanity.

The pastor's commitment to worship is part and parcel of the pastor's commitment to church health. Nothing renews the church like renewing its worship. Nothing affects the lives of individuals more deeply than regularly encountering God in worship. Most pastors accept those truths; but in keeping with the spirit of our times, they are tempted to seek shortcuts for getting there. This is pointless and is the fuel that stokes the fires of the worship wars. What is worth doing is worth doing right. And doing worship begins with the knowledge that God himself has called us to do it. Thus God stands willing to be our partner in transforming venture. Daniel Frankforter points out that "if a congregation's worship seems listless and meaningless, the solution is not to bring on the clowns and magicians to make the corpse dance. It is not to raise a clamorous storm of intoxicating praise noise to cover the death rattle. Hope lies in taking the third person of the Trinity seriously."[1]

The worship renewal movement has, unfortunately, brought with it opportunists hawking a truckload of instant-success approaches. They prey on those looking for an easy way to spike attendance or silence critics. Dealing directly with the Holy Spirit is likely to take longer and be far more costly in a number of ways, but such an approach will have the imprimatur of God, something no one can buy.

## GROWTH VERSUS GRATIFICATION

The reforming of a church and its worship will not be achieved solely through a humanly devised self-help program. No single strategy can be expected to work in every case, for each Christian community's resources and challenges are different. What each needs to grow and flourish is not so much a plan, but a will—to explore, to improvise and to adapt under the guidance of the Holy Spirit.[2]

Among the most strategically important roles of a pastor is to help a congregation determine how, with the Spirit's help, it will marshal its resources and address the challenges of worship in its particular community. For some, this will mean making only minor adjustments. For other churches, this will entail wholesale changes that will stretch the congregation in ways that are uncomfortable. The end is worth the risk.

The temptation to resort to shortcuts and gimmicks is real. But it is possible to win a worship battle yet lose the war. Pastors and congregations that sacrifice their theological or spiritual integrity for the sake of increasing attendance, quieting critics, or resolving disputes within the church will lose in the end. Now more than ever we must resist the siren call of a media-intoxicated culture and refuse to simply give people what they want or gratify merely their felt needs. The real problem with the current culture is that it insulates people from knowing what they most need. As the resident theologian, the pastor must be willing to hold firm to the truth, finding ways to present the gospel to a new generation.

This will entail having a clear conception of what it means to worship in a contemporary fashion. A service of worship that helps people escape the world in which they live is mere entertainment— the liturgical equivalent of a novel or costume drama. Worship that is truly contemporary will, to use a biblical metaphor, turn the world's ferment into a new wine. This new wine will require new wineskins, but the Bible's comparison of faith with wine suggests that truly contemporary is never merely new. Contemporary worship is the celebration of an ancient faith built on enduring principles.[3]

The gospel of Jesus Christ is amenable to a number of "containers," but it must always remain the gospel. Os Guinness said that "the gospel is the best news ever because it addresses our human condition appropriately, pertinently, and effectively as nothing else has, does, or can. And in generation after generation, culture after culture, and life after life."[4] The content of our worship must not, indeed cannot, change. If we let go of the gospel, it will not matter, in the long run, how culturally relevant we are. Karl Barth said, "What matters most in the church's worship is not being up to date, but *reformation.* Reformation does not mean to go with the times or let the spirit of the age judge what is true or false, it means to carry out better than yesterday the task of singing a new song unto the Lord."[5]

## THE ANCIENT FUTURE

Christian worship is timeless. It transcends every age and culture in which it finds itself. This is the design of the God who calls us to worship. On the one hand, our worship builds on practices that stretch back into antiquity. A second-century Christian who walked into a modern church would be completely baffled by the architecture, the musical instruments, sound systems, and backlit screens. But the moment we began to celebrate the Eucharist, he or she would know exactly what we were doing. Our faith, no matter how contemporary the setting, is rooted in the history of Israel, Jesus, and the early church.

At the same time, our faith is more futuristic than the most imaginative science fiction. The visions of John the Revelator reveal a redeemed church, unified in worship. And every Sunday, or whenever the body of Christ gathers for worship, there is a distinctly eschatological flavor that permeates our gatherings like incense. The worship of the church is anticipatory, a weekly dress rehearsal of that day when all of God's people, of "every kindred, every tribe," will gather to invoke eternal adoration and praise. Theologian James Alison writes that "this eschatological approach to worship has the effect of helping the loss of [the Beast's] transcendence, because you can have a party in its face."[6]

Worship is not the innocuous, escapist activity of weak-minded people. Rather it is the daring act of the people of God, living in accordance with their vision of the future. To worship is to party in the face of the Beast. Because it is anticipatory, our worship appears to others to fly in the face of reality. As Alison says, "the old regime hasn't yet heard the news of its own fall."[7] Remember that, the next time someone implies that Christian worship is a flight from reality. To the contrary, our worship services, which proclaim Jesus is Lord, are one of the few places where reality is revealed.

So worship is a case of going back to the future. We are rooted in a salvation history that forms the content of all we say and do as worshipers. But our worship betrays an understanding of the future in which God's sovereign will reigns supreme and His love conquers all. In that sense, the future is already accomplished. Christ is risen. His wedding feast has begun. There is nothing we or anyone else can do about it. It's history, as they say.[8]

That is why weekly worship is an experience of theological déjà vu. Yes, we have been here before, along with all those who have come before us. And if God so wills, the church of future ages will share in this sense of covering old ground in new ways. The opportunity to bring people into the Kingdom, to share with them the future of the church, and to see their lives transformed by that vision makes the weekly treadmill of worship planning eminently worthwhile. Yes, the week does seem to go too quickly sometimes, but the anticipation of assuming the priestly role and mediating God's presence to people in worship is a privilege like few others. That is why, in spite of the pressures and trials of church life, we can't wait for Sunday. For then, if we remain close enough to God, enough in tune with the culture, and hopeful enough of the coming Kingdom, we may lead God's people in a dress rehearsal of the great worship gathering that will take place when His Son returns to lead us before His throne.

Even so, Lord Jesus, come.

# NOTES

—〰—

## PREFACE

1. *A-theism* is the phenomenon in which people claim an intellectual belief in God, but that belief makes no difference in the way they conduct their lives.

2. Don E. Saliers, *Worship As Theology* (Nashville: Abingdon, 1994), 15.

3. Simone Weil, quoted in Guinness, *Prophetic Untimeliness: A Challenge to the Idol of Relevance* (Grand Rapids, Mich.: Baker, 2003), 105.

4. Marva J. Dawn, *A Royal "Waste" of Time* (Grand Rapids, Mich.: Eerdmans, 1999), 146.

## CHAPTER ONE

1. Alan Wolfe, *The Transformation of American Religion* (New York: Free Press, 2003), 2–3.

2. Guinness, *Prophetic Untimeliness*, 65–66 (see intro., n. 2).

3. Steve Mullet, "Quick Quote," *Current Thoughts And Trends* 10, No. 3 (March 1994), 20. Quoted in Marva J. Dawn, *Reaching Out Without Dumbing Down* (Grand Rapids, Mich.: Eerdmans, 1995), 228.

4. Wolfe, *The Transformation of American Religion*, 29.

5. Robb Redman, *The Great Worship Awakening* (San Francisco: Jossey-Bass, 2002), 159.

6. Wolfe, *The Transformation of American Religion*, 32.

7. Guinness, *Prophetic Untimeliness*, 106 (see intro., n. 2).

8. Redman, *The Great Worship Awakening*, 166.

9. Tex Sample, *The Spectacle of Worship* (Nashville: Abingdon, 1998), 105.

10. Marva J. Dawn, *Reaching Out Without Dumbing Down* (Grand Rapids, Mich.: Eerdmans, 1995), 58.

11. Don E. Saliers, *Worship Come to Its Senses* (Nashville: Abingdon, 1996), 78.

12. Dawn, *Reaching Out,* 124.

13. Ibid., 64.

14. Ibid., 141.

## CHAPTER TWO

1. James F. White, quoted in Redman, *The Great Worship Awakening*, 174 (see chap. 1, n. 5).

2. Robert Webber, *Worship Old and New* (Grand Rapids, Mich.: Zondervan, 1994), 262.

3. C. S. Lewis, *Reflections On The Psalms* (New York: Harcourt Brace, 1958), 94. Quoted in Thomas Long, *Testimony: Talking Ourselves into Being Christian* (San Francisco: Jossey-Bass, 2004), 33.

4. Saliers, *Worship As Theology*, 42 (see intro., n. 2).

5. Thomas G. Long, *Beyond the Worship Wars: Building Vital and Faithful Congregations* (Herndon, Va.: The Alban Institute, 2001), 16–17.

6. *The Oxford English Dictionary*, Vol. Xii V-Z (Oxford: Clarendon Press, 1933), 320-321. Cited in David Peterson, *Engaging with God: A Biblical Theology of Worship* (Westmont, Ill.: InterVarsity, 1992), 55.

7. Ibid., 26.

8. Ibid., 19.

9. Ibid., 73.

10. Ibid., 285.

11. Ibid., 206.

12. Ibid., 219.

13. Webber, *Worship Old and New*, 27–28.

14. James Alison, "Worship in a Violent World: A Talk for Ceiliuradh." Dublin, 16 June, 2003 http://www.cccdub.ie/conference/ceiliuradh-2-alison.html.

15. James F. White, *New Forms Of Worship* (Nashville: Abingdon 1971), 32. Quoted in William H. Willimon, *Worship as Pastoral Care* (Nashville: Abingdon, 1979), 21.

16. Ibid., 24.

17. Stanley Hauerwas, *A Community of Character* (Notre Dame, Ind.: The University of Notre Dame Press, 1981), 10.

## CHAPTER THREE

1. Lamin Sanneh, *Translating The Message: The Missionary Impact On Culture,* (Maryknoll: Orbis Books, 1989), 46. Quoted in Dawn, *Reaching Out*, 58 (see chap. 1, n. 10).

2. Eugene Peterson, *The Message,* (Colorado Springs: NavPress, 2002), 1197, 1199.

3. Donald Bloesch, *The Church: Sacraments, Worship, Ministry, and*

*Mission* (Westmont, Ill.: InterVarsity, 2002), 133–34.

4. Redman, *The Great Worship Awakening*, 150 (see chap. 1, n. 5).

5. Thomas G. Long, *Beyond the Worship Wars: Building Vital and Faithful Congregations* (Herndon, Va.: The Alban Institute, 2001), 48.

6. Bloesch, *The Church*, 136–37.

7. Theodore Jennings, *Life As Worship: Prayer And Praise In Jesus's Name* (Grand Rapids: Wm. B. Eerdmans, 1982), 35. Quoted in Saliers, *Worship As Theology*, 111 (see intro., n. 2).

8. Long, *Beyond Worship Wars*, 32.

9. Brian McClaren, *A Generous Orthodoxy* (Grand Rapids, Mich.: Zondervan, 2004), 107.

10. Geoffrey Wainwright, *Doxology: The Praise of God in Worship, Doctrine, and Life* (New York: Oxford, 1980), 35.

## Chapter Four

1. Marva Dawn, *Reaching Out Without Dumbing Down* (Grand Rapids: Wm. B Eerdmans, 1995), 262. Cited in Daniel A. Frankforter, *Stones for Bread: A Critique of Contemporary Worship* (Louisville: Westminster, 2001), 146.

2. Cited in Guinness, *Prophetic Untimeliness*, 74 (see intro., n. 2).

3. Guinness, *Prophetic Untimeliness*, 36 (see intro., n. 2).

4. William H. Willimon, *Worship as Pastoral Care* (Nashville: Abingdon, 1979), 47.

5. Ibid., 18.

6. Ibid., 196.

7. C. S. Lewis, quoted in Willimon, *Worship as Pastoral Care*, 17.

8. Long, *Beyond the Worship Wars*, 18ff. (see chap. 2, n. 5).

9. Dawn, *Reaching Out*, 78 (see chap. 1, n. 10).

10. Terri Bocklund McLean, *New Harmonies: Choosing Contemporary Music for Worship* (Herndon, Va.: The Alban Institute, 1998), 87.

11. Long, *Beyond the Worship Wars*, 97 (see chap. 2, n. 5).

12. Ibid., 99–100.

13. Ibid., 100–103.

14. Daniel A. Frankforter, *Stones for Bread: A Critique of Contemporary Worship* (Louisville: Westminster, 2001), 175–76.

## Chapter Five

1. Paul Basden, *The Worship Maze: Finding a Style to Fit Your Church* (Westmont, Ill.: InterVarsity, 1999), 36.

2. James F. White, *Introduction to Christian Worship* (Nashville: Abingdon, 1990), 31–32.

3. Cited in Dawn, *Reaching Out*, 82 (see chap. 1, n. 10).

4. Ibid., 82.

5. Carlton R. Young, quoted in White, *Introduction to Christian Worship*, 114.

6. Redman, *The Great Worship Awakening*, 39 (see chap. 1, n. 5).

7. White, *Introduction to Christian Worship,* 163.

8. Saliers, *Worship Come to Its Senses*, 73 (see chap. 1, n. 11).

9. Brad Berglund, *Reinventing Sunday: Breakthrough Ideas for Transforming Worship* (Valley Forge, Pa.: Judson, 2001), 16.

10. Ibid., 5–6.

11. Saliers, *Worship As Theology*, 27 (see intro., n. 2).

12. Dawn, *A Royal "Waste" of Time*, 154 (see intro., n. 4).

13. Sally Morganthaler, *Worship Evangelism* (Grand Rapids, Mich.: Zondervan, 1995), 17.

14. Cited in Dawn, *Reaching Out,* 20–24 (see chap. 1, n. 10).

15. Saliers, *Worship As Theology,* 86 (see intro., n. 2).

16. Robert Webber, *Planning Blended Worship* (Nashville: Abingdon, 1998), 122.

17. Paul Hoon, *The Integrity Of Worship: Ecumenical And Pastoral Studies In Liturgical Theology*, (Nashville: Abingdon, 1971). Quoted in Saliers, *Worship As Theology,* 154 (see intro., n. 2).

18. Webber, *Blended Worship*, 23.

19. Ibid., 100.

20. Frankforter, *Stones for Bread*, 95 (see chap. 4, n. 14).

21. Ibid., xii.

## CHAPTER SIX

1. Morganthaler, *Worship Evangelism*, 92 (see chap. 5, n. 13).

2. David Wells, *No Place for Truth* (Grand Rapids, Mich.: Eerdmans, 1993), 145.

3. Long, *Beyond the Worship Wars*, 3 (see chap. 2, n. 5).

4. Ibid., 8.

5. Redman, *The Great Worship Awakening*, 161 (see chap. 1, n. 5).

6. Frankforter, *Stones for Bread*, 170 (see chap. 4, n. 14).

7. Dawn, *Reaching Out*, 266 (see chap. 1, n. 10).

8. William H. Willimon, *With Glad and Generous Hearts* (Nashville:

Upper Room, 1986), 57.

9. Walter Brueggemann, *The Message of the Psalms* (Minneapolis: Augsburg, 1984), 51.

10. Saliers, *Worship As Theology*, 135 (see intro., n. 2).

11. Ibid., 121.

12. Saliers, *Worship Come to Its Senses*, 56 (see chap. 1, n. 11).

13. Willimon, *With Glad and Generous Hearts*, 43.

14. Webber, *Planning Blended Worship*, 112 (see chap. 5, n. 16).

15. Robert Webber, *"The Convergence Movement,"* in *The Christian Century,* 1982 99 (3) quoted in Redman, *The Great Worship Awakening*, 79–80 (see chap. 1, n. 5).

## CHAPTER SEVEN

1. Long, *Beyond the Worship Wars*, 2 (see chap. 2, n. 5).

2. Ibid., 11.

3. Ibid.

4. Dan Kimball, *Emerging Worship* (Grand Rapids, Mich.: Zondervan, 2004), xiv.

5. Leonard Sweet, *Postmodern Pilgrims* (Nashville: Broadman, 2000), xxi.

6. Webber, *Planning Blended Worship*, 17–19 (see chap. 5, n. 16).

7. Brian McClaren, quoted in Dan Kimball, *Emerging Worship*, 9.

## CHAPTER EIGHT

1. Joseph Cardinal Bernardin, *The Collegville Hymnal*, 7. Quoted in Berglund, *Reinventing Sunday*, 28 (see chap. 5, n. 9).

2. White, *Introduction to Christian Worship*, 111 (see chap. 5., n. 2).

3. Dietrich Bonhoeffer, *Life Together* (San Francisco: HarperCollins Publishers, 1954), 59.

4. Joseph Sittler, "Dogma And Doxa," *Worship: Good News In Action*, Ed. Mandus A. Egge (Minneapolis: Augsburg, 1973), 23. Quoted in Saliers, *Worship As Theology*, 40 (see intro., n. 2).

5. Calvin M. Johansson, *Discipling Music Ministry* (Peabody, Mass.: Hendrickson, 1992), 13.

6. Ibid., 1.

7. Ibid., 2ff.

8. Dawn, *Reaching Out*, 170ff. (see chap. 1, n. 10).

9. Samuel Adler, quoted in Paul Westermeyer, *Professional Concerns*

*Forum: Chant, Bach, and Popular Culture, The American Organist* 27 no. 11 (Nov. 1993): 35, quoted in Dawn, *Reaching Out*, 166 (see chap. 1, n. 10).

10. Johansson, *Discipling Music Ministry*, 7ff.

11. Ibid., 49.

12. Redman, *The Great Worship Awakening*, 199 (see chap. 1, n. 5).

13. Brian Wren, *Praying Twice: The Music and Words of Congregational Songs* (Louisville: Westminster, 2000), 135ff.

14. Ibid., 135.

15. Ibid., 140.

16. Dawn, *Reaching Out*, 181 (see chap. 1, n. 10).

17. Johansson, *Discipling Music Ministry*, 108.

18. Robert Webber, *Enter His Courts with Praise: A Study of the Role of Music and the Arts in Worship* (Peabody, Mass.: Hendrickson, 1997), 53.

19. Ibid., 54.

20. Wren, *Praying Twice*, 52.

21. Ibid., 53.

22. Andy Crouch, "Amplified Versions," *Christianity Today*, April 23, 2002, 86.

23. Robin Leaver, *The Theological Character Of Music In Worship* (St. Louis: Concordia, 1989), 17. Quoted in Bocklund McLean, *New Harmonies*, 103 (see chap. 4, n. 10).

24. Johansson, *Discipling Music Ministry*, 146.

25. Ibid., 146.

26. Webber, *Enter His Courts with Praise*, 51.

27. Frankforter, *Stones for Bread*, 112ff. (see chap. 4, n. 14).

28. Webber, *Enter His Courts with Praise*, 43–44.

29. Wren, *Praying Twice*, 159–160.

30. Ibid., 160.

31. Ibid., 1.

32. For a fuller treatment of this topic, see Johansson, *Discipling Music Ministry*, 128–31.

33. Bocklund McLean, *New Harmonies*, 99 (see chap. 4, n. 10).

## CHAPTER NINE

1. Long, *Beyond the Worship Wars*, 62–63 (see chap. 2, n. 5).

2. Bocklund McLean, *New Harmonies*, 15 (see chap. 4, n. 10).

3. Ibid., 19.

4. Wren, *Praying Twice*, 71 (see chap. 8, n. 13).

5. Bocklund McLean, *New Harmonies*, 61 (see chap. 4, n. 10).

6. Redman, *The Great Worship Awakening*, 64–65 (see chap. 1, n. 5).

7. Long, *Beyond the Worship Wars*, 64 (see chap. 2, n. 5).

8. Redman, *The Great Worship Awakening*, 190 (see chap. 1, n. 5).

9. Wren, *Praying Twice*, 110–12 (see chap. 8, n. 13).

10. Webber, *Planning Blended Worship*, 16 (see chap. 5, n. 16).

11. Leonard Sweet, *Faithquakes* (Nashville: Abingdon, 1994), 67. Quoted in Bocklund McLean, *New Harmonies*, 113 (see chap. 4, n. 10).

12. Ibid., 103.

13. Long, *Beyond the Worship Wars*, 61 (see chap. 2, n. 5).

14. Wren, *Praying Twice*, 84–96 (see chap. 8, n. 13).

15. Ibid., 75–76.

## CHAPTER TEN

1. Long, *Beyond the Worship Wars*, 43 (see chap. 2, n. 5).

2. Webber, *Enter His Courts*, 3 (see chap. 8, n. 18).

3. White, *Introduction to Christian Worship*, 117 (see chap. 5, n. 2).

4. William B. Hendricks, *Exit Interviews* (Chicago: Moody Press, 1993), 196. Quoted in Dawn, *Reaching Out Without Dumbing Down*, 195 (see intro, n 4).

5. Redman, *The Great Worship Awakening*, 208 (see chap. 1, n. 5).

6. Webber, *Enter His Courts,* 79 (see chap. 8, n. 18).

7. Frankforter, *Stones for Bread*, 158 (see chap. 4, n. 14).

8. White, *Introduction to Christian Worship*, 89 (see chap. 5, n. 2).

9. Long, *Beyond the Worship Wars*, 65 (see chap. 2, n. 5).

10. White, *Introduction to Christian Worship*, 90 (see chap. 5, n. 2).

11. Ibid., 88–121.

12. Dawn, *A Royal "Waste" of Time*, 155 (see intro., n. 4).

13. Long, *Beyond the Worship Wars*, 67 (see chap. 2, n. 5).

14. Wainwright, *Doxology*, 393 (see chap. 3, n. 9).

## CHAPTER ELEVEN

1. Long, *Beyond the Worship Wars*, 17–18 (see chap. 2, n. 5).

2. Webber, *Planning Blended Worship*, 21 (see chap. 5, n. 16).

3. Ibid., 22.

4. Ibid.

5. Ibid., 42.

**CHAPTER TWELVE**

1. White, *Introduction to Christian Worship*, 162 (see chap. 5, n. 2).

2. Ruth C. Duck, *Finding Words for Worship* (Louisville: Westminster, 1995), 130.

**CHAPTER THIRTEEN**

1. Peterson, *Engaging with God*, 18–19 (see chap. 2, n. 6).

2. Thomas G. Long, *Testimony: Talking Ourselves into Being Christian* (San Francisco: Jossey-Bass, 2004), 48.

3. Peterson, *Engaging with God*, 286 (see chap. 2, n. 6).

4. Wainwright, *Doxology*, 422 (see chap. 3, n. 9).

5. Long, *Testimony*, 40.

6. Ibid., 135.

7. A. W. Tozer, *The Pursuit Of God* (Camp Hill, Pa: Christian Publications, 1982) 17-18. Quoted in Morganthaler, *Worship Evangelism*, 35 (see chap. 5, n. 13).

8. Long, *Testimony,* 65.

**CHAPTER FOURTEEN**

1. John D. Witvliet, *Worship Seeking Understanding* (Grand Rapids, Mich.: Baker, 2003), 279.

2. Dawn, *Reaching Out*, 218–19 (see chap. 1, n. 10).

3. Ibid., 216.

4. Witvliet, *Worship Seeking Understanding*, 283–84.

**CHAPTER FIFTEEN**

1. Frankforter, *Stones for Bread*, 184.

2. Ibid., 165–66.

3. Ibid., 14.

4. Guinness, *Prophetic Untimeliness*, 13 (see intro., n. 3).

5. Karl Barth, *Church Dogmatics* Vol. 4, Part 1 (New York: Charles Scribner's Sons, 1956) 705. Quoted in William H. Willimon, *Word, Water, Wine and Bread* (Valley Forge, Pa.: Judson, 1980), 6.

6. James Alison, "Worship in a Violent World" (see chap. 2, n. 14).

7. Ibid.

8. Ibid.

# SELECTED BIBLIOGRAPHY

—꿈—

Berglund, Brad. *Reinventing Sunday: Breakthrough Ideas for Transforming Worship.* Valley Forge, Pa: Judson Press, 2001.

Bocklund McLean, Terri. *New Harmonies: Choosing Contemporary Music for Worship.* Herndon, Va.: The Alban Institute, 1998.

Dawn, Marva J. *A Royal "Waste" of Time.* Grand Rapids, Mich.: Eerdmans, 1999.

———. *Reaching Out Without Dumbing Down.* Grand Rapids, Mich.: Eerdmans, 1995.

Duck, Ruth C. *Finding Words for Worship.* Louisville: Westminster, 1995.

Kimball, Dan. *Emerging Worship.* Grand Rapids, Mich.: Zondervan, 2004.

Long, Thomas G. *Beyond the Worship Wars: Building Vital and Faithful Congregations.* Herndon, Va.: The Alban Institute, 2001.

Morgenthaler, Sally. *Worship Evangelism.* Grand Rapids, Mich.: Zondervan, 1995.

Peterson, David. *Engaging God: A Biblical Theology of Worship.* Westmont, Ill.: InterVarsity, 1992.

Redman, Robb. *The Great Worship Awakening.* San Francisco: Jossey-Bass, 2002.

Saliers, Don E. *Worship As Theology.* Nashville: Abingdon, 1994.

Sample, Tex. *The Spectacle of Worship in a Wired World.* Nashville: Abingdon, 1998.

Wainwright, Geoffrey. *Doxology: The Praise of God in Worship, Doctrine, and Life.* New York: Oxford, 1980

Webber, Robert. *Blended Worship: Achieving Substance and Relevance in Worship.* Peabody, Mass.: Hendrickson, 1994.

———. *Enter His Courts with Praise: A Study of the Role of Music and the Arts in Worship.* Peabody, Mass.: Hendrickson, 1997.

————. *Worship Old and New*. Grand Rapids, Mich.: Zondervan, 1994.

————. *The Younger Evangelicals*. Grand Rapids, Mich.: Baker Books, 2002.

White, James F. *Introduction to Christian Worship*. Nashville: Abingdon, 1990.

Willimon, William H. *Pastor: The Theology and Practice of Ordained Ministry*. Nashville: Abingdon, 2002.

————. *With Glad and Generous Hearts*. Nashville: Upper Room, 1986.

————. *Worship as Pastoral Care*. Nashville: Abingdon, 1979.

Wren, Brian. *Praying Twice: The Music and Words of Congregational Songs*. Louisville: Westminster, 2000.